COLLINS GEM

FOOD
FOR
MICROWAVING

Lorna Rhodes
Consultant: Ann Nicol

HarperCollins*Publishers*

HarperCollins Publishers
P.O. Box, Glasgow G4 0NB

First published 1992
© 1992 The Book Creation Company
Reprint 10 9 8 7 6 5 4 3 2 1 0

ISBN 0 00 458990 4

Printed in Great Britain by
HarperCollins Manufacturing, Glasgow

Introduction

The Collins Gem Food for Microwaving is an easy-to-use reference book. It provides a comprehensive guide to how your microwave works, hints and tips on microwave cooking techniques and entries on cookware best suited to microwave cooking. It provides an accessible and valuable introduction to microwave cookery. Common foodstuffs are listed alphabetically and in each entry clear explanations are given on how to prepare and cook the food in a microwave, as well as listing those foods not suitable for microwaving and why.

The cooking information is given in general terms because there are many considerations that have to be taken into account when using your microwave. Always consult the manufacturer's handbook and become familiar with your model, the way it operates and the functions it offers. It is important to know the wattage of your oven; most domestic microwave ovens are within the 600–700 W range. Depending on the wattage of an oven cooking times will have to be either increased or shortened. The cooking times in this guide are for a 650 W oven.

The majority of the cooking times given are for cooking food on High, which is the same as Full or 100%. The cooking time depends on the weight of the food, so obviously the more food you cook the longer it takes. The times are not given exactly (4–5 minutes) to allow for a variety of conditions; for instance, food that is very cold will take a little longer to cook, and the kind of dish the food is cooked in may also affect the cooking time. It is always best to check the food at the shortest cooking time. If it is slightly undercooked it can easily be cooked a little longer, but nothing can be done to rescue overcooked food.

The Appendices have several tables that give a quick, easy reference to cooking times, defrosting times and reheating times for the majority of foods.

Commercially prepared foods, such as chilled or frozen meals, should be cooked according to the directions given by the manufacturer on the label or pack. These products have been thoroughly tested and the times given will ensure that the food is properly heated to avoid any risk of food poisoning. Always check what wattage oven the cooking times refer to.

The Collins Gem Food for Microwaving is thoroughly cross-referenced with the cross-references appearing in **bold lettering**.

Why use a microwave?

The busy lives we lead today means that food must be prepared quickly and conveniently.

This has been reflected in the great increase in the availability and variety of ready-prepared meals.

In addition, with the growing emphasis in healthy eating, fitness and travel, there has been a revolution in the style of food and types of meals eaten in recent years. The trend in eating ethnic food looks likely to increase, while the demand for fresh, healthy ingredients will also be a priority for many people.

Using a microwave not only reduces drastically cooking time as compared to conventional methods, but it also uses far less energy. So whether preparing a home-made dish or heating a ready-made meal, the microwave saves time, energy and money. It has become an invaluable and integral part of the modern kitchen.

Microwave cooking is also a very healthy way of cooking food. Less fats, oils and liquids are needed, therefore the nutrients are retained in the food. The shape, colour, flavour and texture of the food is maintained because it is cooked much more quickly than in other methods. As well as the convenience of quick cooking the microwave can offer speedy defrosting and reheating, which are essential requirements in a hectic household. It is also an easier way of cooking for single people. It is a perfect way of cooking single portions with minimum effort and involves far less washing up.

The microwave is easy to clean and above all safe to use. Children, the elderly and disabled can use it without risk of burning themselves on a hot element or naked flame. Microwave ovens stay cool during cooking and have to meet high international standards for the mechanical and electrical safety. There is less risk of food boiling over or burning, because it will cook for a specified period only and then switch itself off.

However, just because the microwave is so quick and simple to use, it does not follow that only quick and simple recipes must be used. It can be used for more than just heating prepared meals. The microwave is ideal when entertaining and many different cooking stages need to be completed, for example melting chocolate, dissolving gelatin or making sauces. All these tasks can be more easily carried out in the microwave oven. In conjunction with the freezer the microwave can help extensively with the preparations for a special occasion.

Microwave ovens have the advantage that they can be easily moved and used in other parts of the house if required. All domestic cookers run off a 13 amp socket outlet and, as long as the microwave is not fitted into a housing unit, it can be moved to another room in the house, or even (with an extension reel) used outside to help prepare food for an outdoor meal.

Having given many of the advantages of microwave cookery it must be recognised that microwave cooking involves quite different techniques compared with the traditional methods of cooking. Often problems arise because the cook does not get involved enough with the cooking process and expects the machine to do everything. Just as in conventional cooking, when preparing food in a microwave it is turned, stirred and checked. It takes skill to master the techniques and there is always an element of trial and error to begin with, just as there is with any new piece of kitchen equipment. Do not expect to master microwave cooking techniques immediately; it takes practice to get perfect results, so start with simple dishes before attempting more complicated recipes.

Once the basics of how the microwave works are grasped, the benefits it can offer far outweigh its limitations.

Choosing a microwave oven

The first feature to consider when choosing an oven will be its size or internal capacity. This can vary from the compact 0.4 cubic feet to 1.3 cubic feet. Often the smaller models are bought for the sole purpose of reheating food and usually operate at a lower wattage. They can also, however, be ideal for cooking for one or two.

An average family will find a 0.9–1.3 cubic feet oven more suitable, because they can accommodate larger items of cookware and bulky foods.

The most popular types of microwave are the free-standing models, which sit on the worktop. There are some microwave ovens that can be incorporated into housing units where the microwave acts as a second cooker and works independently of the conventional oven. Combination ovens can operate as conventional cookers and microwave ovens, using both types of power simultaneously. These are increasing in popularity despite being quite expensive. They offer many sophisticated features, such as fans to circulate the hot air so that the food is cooked more quickly and ways to improve the browning and crispness of food. It is essential to know the wattage output of the oven. Microwave ovens can range from 400–700 W. High-wattage ovens cook faster than low wattage ovens. The most popular oven wattage is 650 W.

Variable power levels allow the cooking power to be adjusted to give better results. On average five options will be offered, but some models can have up to 10 power levels. Ovens may have manual or digital controls. Digital displays are preferable because they are more accurate, especially for cooking processes that require only seconds.

Before choosing a microwave there are some other features worth considering, for example, automatic programmes can help eliminate guesswork in estimating cooking times. These work by a sensor system and manufacturers are improving these all the time. To use the automatic cooking function the type of food to be cooked is selected from the food categories offered on the controls on the front of the oven. The oven then automatically chooses the correct power level and the amount of cooking time. Some models have a 'more-or-less' pad, which allows greater control over the cooking. Humidity sensors detect the build up of steam either in the oven capacity or under the food covering. This method works best with foods that have a high water content. Weight sensors work by calculating the cooking time on the basis of the food's weight. These tend to be used on a limited range of food, such as a joint or whole chicken. Automatic controls can also include variations for reheating and defrosting.

Many cookers incorporate a turntable instead of or in addition to the wave stirrer. This helps to distribute the microwaves evenly through the cooker, therefore ensuring that the food is cooked evenly. There are some models available with a browning element, but because the interior of the ovens cannot withstand the heat of grills these are usually rated at only 1000 W, and do not work as well as conventional grills. Combination ovens are often fitted with a grill and these models do work more efficiently.

Before choosing a microwave oven it is best to research the latest models on the market, send off for brochures and visit a store where demonstrations take place and actually see microwave ovens in action. Each microwave will offer a different combination of features and it is a matter of deciding which model will suit you particular needs. Many microwave ovens have been known to be bought entirely on their colour, but white is still the most popular choice.

How a microwave oven works

A microwave is basically a metal box containing an electronic device called a magnetron. This converts ordinary household electrical energy into electromagnetic waves, which move at high speed within the cooker as they are deflected off the metal walls of the oven cavity. Microwaves penetrate the food from all directions to a depth of up to 4 cm. The microwaves are absorbed by the molecules of moisture in the food causing them to vibrate rapidly, which produces the heat that cooks the food. The molecules vibrate many thousands of times a second, producing a very intense heat.

The centre of the food is cooked by conduction as in conventional cooking. Microwaves do not cause any structural or chemical change in the food.

Microwave cooking is determined by the amount of microwave energy (which depends on the wattage of the model), the length of time the food is in the oven and by the quantity, shape and type of food.

The cooker door and door frame are fitted with special seals to ensure that the microwaves are safely contained within the cooker. All microwaves have a cut-out device so that the flow of microwave energy stops automatically and immediately whenever the door is opened.

Microwaves can pass through glass, pottery, china, paper and most plastics, so these materials make ideal cooking containers. As metals reflect microwaves, food cannot be cooked in foil, metallic containers or dishes with a gold or silver decoration.

Guidelines for successful cooking

As with any new item of kitchen equipment, read the manufacturer's instruction book carefully before using, and use its hints and recipes until you are confident about how your model works. As a general guide, microwaving takes about a third to a quarter of conventional cooking time. The more food you cook at one time the longer it takes. When doubling a microwave recipe, allow a third to a half extra time. When halving a recipe try two-thirds to three-quarters of the original time. Always allow for standing time when a recipe gives it as this is part of the cooking time. The heat within the food continues to cook it even when it has been removed from the oven.

Keep food moist by covering it with a lid, a plate or some microwave film. Clingfilm is useful, but make sure it does not come into contact with the food and pierce or fold back a little to allow steam to escape. You must use only clingfilm that is specially designed for use in a microwave – never use ordinary clingfilm.

Fat will spatter from some foods, such as sausages and bacon, so it is a good idea to cover them with absorbent paper before cooking. Foods that are most successfully cooked in a microwave are those that would normally be cooked by moist methods similar to poaching, steaming, stewing or braising. Foods that need crisping and drying in a hot oven, under a grill or in fat, such as rich pastry, toast, chips and pancakes are not successful when cooked in the microwave. In any case, deep frying should never be attempted because it would be too dangerous.

Where a specific size or shape of dish is recommended in a recipe, use it or the timing and results may vary from what is intended. Generally, use a larger dish for microwave cooking than conventional cooking and never fill any dish more than two-thirds full. This allows liquids to boil up and provides space for stirring.

The shape of food will also affect the way it cooks in the microwave. In most ovens microwaves are concentrated round the edges with less energy in the centre. This means that foods such as chops or fish should be arranged round the edge of the dish with the thinner parts towards the centre to ensure even cooking. Any food with liquid, such as casseroles and stewed fruit, should be stirred to distribute the heat evenly. In microwave ovens that do not have a turntable, stirrer fan or paddle, the dish will need to be turned or rotated manually during cooking. Where possible try to arrange food so that there is an empty space in the middle, this allows the microwaves to penetrate it from all sides. Stand ramekins in a circle or small portions of food of equal size around the edge of the dish to help cook evenly. Foods in dishes that cannot be stirred or rearranged, such as lasagne, should be given three separate quarter turns during cooking.

Microwave cooking does not brown food, but this can be done in various ways. Some people prefer to complete the cooking in a conventional oven to achieve a crisp, brown finish, particularly this with a large joint of meat or poultry. However, for smaller items of food, such as chops, steak or chicken portions, a browning dish is a good investment. It is made from ceramic and coated with material that absorbs microwave energy. It should be pre-heated without food and when the surface becomes hot it can be used with a little oil or butter. The food is pressed onto the hot surface to cause searing and browning. Alternatively, the pale surface can be disguised by using a browning agent. Paprika, brown sauce, microwave browning mix or seasoning are just a few examples of what can be used to enhance the colour of the food.

Sweet foods, such as cakes and puddings, will often look and taste better if brown sugar and wholemeal flour are used instead of refined white products.

As defrosting and reheating are so quick, a freezer is the ideal complement to a microwave. A little forethought in home-freezing will help when it comes to using the microwave. For example, freeze food in microwave-safe containers so that they can be put straight into the microwave. Freeze food in single or double portions so that the exact quantity can be removed as needed. It is also quicker to thaw several small portions one after another rather than one large frozen mass, which could take a very long time. Cook extra quantities when preparing dishes and freeze what is not required, which can then be microwaved easily at a later date.

When reheating food from the freezer it is always best to thaw it first, because on the whole the texture of the finished product is better and reheats more evenly. When thawing in the microwave it is essential that the ice is melted slowly. If it is not thawed slowly the food begins to cook on the outside before the centre has thawed. Allow food to rest between bursts of microwave energy or use an auto-defrost setting. Cook meat and poultry as soon as it is defrosted. Joints of meat defrosted in the microwave may lose a lot of their juices, pour these off before they start to cook, and if possible stand the meat on a roasting rack to keep it clear of liquid.

When reheating food in the microwave it is very important to ensure that it is piping hot. Place the food in a shallow container so the microwaves can penetrate the food easily. It is best to cover the food because the steam produced will be trapped and helps the heating process. If possible stir the food during reheating and if not shake the dish gently. Do not reheat large pieces of meat, chicken or fish, because if they are not hot enough in the middle the edges will overcook. Fat and sugar attract microwaves and tend to get hotter than other ingredients, so be careful when serving dishes such as fruit pies.

To create new recipes or to adapt favourite recipes for microwave cooking, it is a good idea to find a recipe in a microwave cookbook that has given good results. Use it as a guide for ingredients, weight, suggested containers and cooking times. Then you can add your own variations and create your individual recipes. Remember it is always best to undercook than overcook and allow for standing time.

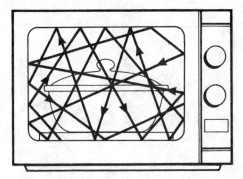

Microwaves bounce off the walls in a regular pattern. They pass through the containers into the food and vibrate the water modules. This causes friction which generates heat.

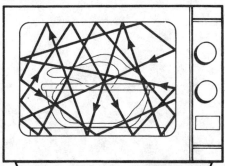

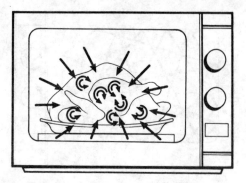

The centre of a large piece of food is cooked by conduction of heat produced near the surface of the food.

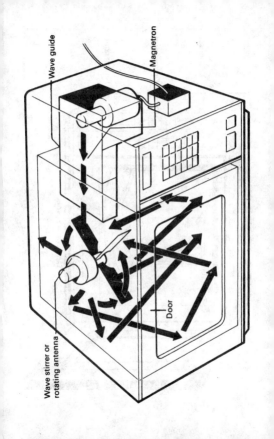

Wave guide

Magnetron

Wave stirrer or rotating antenna

Door

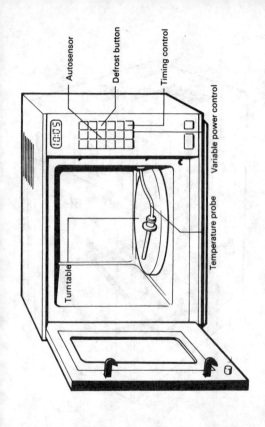

Autosensor

Defrost button

Timing control

Variable power control

Temperature probe

Turntable

absorption Any substance that contains water, fat or sugar soaks up microwave energy and becomes hot. The microwaves make the moisture molecules vibrate at an intense rate, which causes friction and generates heat to cook the food. The microwaves can only penetrate to about 5 cm (2 in), but the food then cooks with one layer heating up the next by conduction.

acorn squash A thick-skinned variety of **squash**, which is available in the autumn. Because it has such a tough skin it is usually cooked unpeeled and often cut into rings.

TO COOK: cut into half, scoop out the seeds and fibres, and place the halves, side by side, in a dish. Cover the dish and cook 225 g on high for 5 minutes, 450 g for 7 minutes. Cooked acorn squash can be added to soups, purées and desserts. See also **fruit**.

adzuki bean A small, reddish-brown, round bean, which has a delicious sweet flavour when cooked. Adzuki beans may be used instead of lentils in soups, salads, bakes or burgers.

TO COOK: after soaking, rinse the beans and place them in a large dish. Fill with fresh boiling water, cook covered on high and for 225 g beans allow 25–30 minutes, stirring 2 or 3 times during cooking, then leave to **stand** for 15–20 minutes. If they are not completely soft, cook for a further 5 minutes and test again. See also **pulses**.

air vent   A series of narrow gaps found on the outside of the microwave oven to allow any steam to escape during cooking. Vents should be kept unobstructed and have at least 5 cm (2 in) of clear space above the oven for air circulation. See also **features of the microwave oven**.

alcohol   The intoxicating, colourless liquid derived from the fermentation of sugars. Many alcoholic drinks are added to dishes, including wine, whisky and rum. However, care must be taken when cooking with alcohol in the microwave. The recipe used must be followed strictly because if the food is allowed to overheat it may explode.

Reheat **Christmas pudding** and **mince pies** for a few seconds at a time. Brandy may be warmed in the microwave for a few seconds to help ignite it when poured over a Christmas pudding.

allspice   The whole or powdered seeds of a tropical American tree, used as a spice. Allspice tastes like a mixture of cinnamon, nutmeg and cloves. Most allspice comes from Jamaica, which is why it is sometimes called Jamaica pepper. It may be used as an alternative to mixed spice in baking, and a few whole berries make an interesting addition to stews and casseroles.

almond The oval-shaped, nutlike fruit of a tree of West Asian origin. Sweet almonds can be bought whole, or shelled with their skins removed as either blanched, flaked, nibbed or ground. They are best known for their use in sweets and in baking.

TO BLANCH: place 250 ml of water in a jug, cook on high for $2\frac{1}{2}$ minutes or until boiling, add the almonds and cook for $\frac{1}{2}$ minute. Drain and slip the skins off. See also **nuts**.

aluminium foil See **foil**.

anchovy A small **fish** belonging to the herring family (similar to a sardine), which is usually filleted and cured, by salting or brining, and then canned or bottled. Because they are very salty, cured anchovies are only used in small amounts in dishes. Fresh anchovies are not readily available, they also have a strong flavour, but are not as salty as cured ones. Anchovy essence is a useful flavouring for fish sauces and can be used to enrich beef stews.

aniseed The highly flavoured, aromatic seeds of the Mediterranean anise plant. These small seeds have a taste similar to liquorice, and may be used to flavour food, such as chicken dishes. They will benefit from being toasted first before being used.

apple A firm-fleshed **fruit**. There are many varieties of apple; dessert or eating apples have more flavour then cooking apples, each with their own distinctive taste. Cooking apples are too tart to eat on their own, but are delicious cooked with sugar.

TO COOK: peel, core and slice, then sprinkle with lemon juice and a little sugar or honey. Cover and cook on high allowing 3–4 minutes for 225 g and 5–6 minutes for 450 g. Allow to **stand** for 3 minutes. To purée apple (to make apple sauce) cook for a further 3 minutes with 1 tbsp of water until the apples slices are soft and collapsed, then mash until smooth.

To cook whole apples, core and fill apples with a mixture of dried fruit and sugar, then score round the centre to prevent bursting. Add 3 tbsp of water, cover, and cook on high: 1 apple (approx. 225 g) for 2–3 minutes; 2 apples 4–5 minutes; 4 apples 7–9 minutes. Rotate the apples halfway through cooking. Allow to stand covered for 2 minutes.

apricot The small, smooth-skinned fruit of the apricot tree, with sweet-tasting flesh. Select firm, unwrinkled fruit with a deep colour. Less perfect fruits are good cooked in vanilla flavoured syrup and can be used in tarts or puréed to use as a sauce, in sorbets, mousses or fools. Apricots are used in savoury recipes in the Middle East and go well with lamb and chickpeas. Wash and dry the fruit and remove any stalks, and when cooking whole prick the skins before poaching in syrup. They may also be halved and stoned before cooking.

TO COOK: either (a), add to syrup, cover and cook 450 g of fruit on high for 4–5 minutes and stir halfway through cooking; or (b), add just 15 ml of apple juice or water to the fruit and cook. Allow to **stand** for 3 minutes. See also **dried fruit**.

arbori (also called **Italian rice**) A short large-grained pearly **rice**, preferred for Italian cooking, particularly risotto.

arcing (also called **sparking**) A term to describe a spark caused when a dish or utensil made of metal, or any form of metal trim, or gold or silver decoration, is used in the microwave. Metal reflects the microwaves and produces a blue spark. If this happens the oven should be switched off immediately as arcing can damage the cooker **magnetron**. Be careful to use **foil** in small amounts for **shielding** and never let it come near, or in contact with, the oven walls. It is best to avoid using foil all together if possible.

arranging food Food has to be arranged carefully to ensure even cooking. It should be cooked in dishes of the appropriate shape and size. Arranging food in a circle with the centre left empty will provide the best results, because this allows the microwaves to penetrate from the centre as well as the outside. Unevenly shaped foods, such as chops, broccoli, asparagus and fish fillets, should be arranged with the thinner or more delicate parts towards the centre. Similarly when cooking different foods together, place denser, slower cooking ingredients near the outer edge of the dish and quicker cooking ones in the middle. Place small dishes or ramekins and items like cupcakes or meatballs in a circle with space in between, and rotate individual items a half turn at least once during cooking. See also **rearranging food**; **reheating**.

asparagus The stem and leaves of the young asparagus plant. There are two basic types of asparagus, blanched (white) and green. Choose stems that look fresh and tender, and avoid wilted stems, ones with brown patches or those that look coarse and woody. Trim off the woody ends, wash, and arrange in a dish with the tender tips pointing towards the centre.

TO COOK: add 4 tbsp of water to 450 g of asparagus, cover and cook on high for 6–7 minutes, rearranging the spears halfway through cooking. Cooking time will vary with the thickness and age of spears.

aspic A savoury jelly made from meat or fish stock, used to coat meats, poultry, fish and vegetables. Aspic can also be layered in a mould with ingredients arranged in attractive designs. For speed and convenience manufactured aspic may be used, which comes in powdered form.

TO COOK: sprinkle aspic powder over liquid in a glass jug and leave until it becomes spongy. Place the jug in the oven and cook on high for 1–2 minutes, stirring until dissolved.

aubergine (also called **eggplant**) The egg-shaped fruit of a tropical Asian plant, with a rich, glossy, purple skin. Select firm aubergines with tight, glossy skins, avoiding any that are wrinkled and bruised. They are best cooked whole, whether they are to be sliced or puréed afterwards, to avoid the flesh turning brown. However, it is often recommended that aubergines are salted before cooking, to draw out any bitter juices. To salt them, place slices or cubes in a colander, sprinkle with salt and leave for 30 minutes before rinsing and drying on kitchen paper.

TO COOK: wipe, or rinse, and dry 2 aubergines (each about 225 g) then trim off the calyx. Cut the aubergines in half, lengthways, and score the flesh in a criss-cross pattern. Place them in the oven, cover with kitchen paper and cook on high for 3–4 minutes. Turn over and rearrange once during cooking. Allow to **stand** for 4 minutes. Serve whole, sliced or mashed.

To cook stuffed aubergines, cook for the minimum time and stand; scoop out the flesh, and mix with other ingredients before replacing in the shell. Reheat for 2–4 minutes. For slices or cubes, place in a dish with 15 ml of oil and cook for the same length of time, and use as a cooked vegetable or in a moussaka.

audible reminder A bell, buzzer or pinger that sounds when the cooking time has been completed.

automatic defrost Automatic programmes eliminate guesswork and are particularly helpful to cooks new to microwaving. Most microwaves have a defrost button and some have automatic defrosting. Microwave energy is pulsed on and off, so that **standing time** is allowed for. This helps to prevent food from starting to cook at the edges before the centre has thawed.

automatic programming A feature that allows more than one setting to be programmed at the same time, so that a number of cooking sequences can be carried out on one setting. This is useful, for example, when cooking casseroles because cooking starts on high and is completed on a lower setting, or when thawing food and then automatically switching to a setting for cooking.

auto-sensor A feature that automatically programmes the power setting and cooking time for a pre-selected range of foods. The type of food chosen will be cooked quite accurately because the microwave can calculate the time required. It measures the air temperature and amount of steam released during cooking. The microwave will switch itself off automatically when the food is done.

To ensure that this works successfully food must be cooked covered, using either a lid or microwave-safe **clingfilm**. Do not open the door during the first stage of cooking, while the steam is building up, because this will cause the sensor to miscalculate. Once in operation the remaining cooking time is displayed. Using the auto-sensor can be very helpful, but generally it takes 10% longer than setting the time and power manually.

avocado pear The pear-shaped fruit of a tropical American plant, with smooth, green or knobbly, black skin. The delicate buttery flesh of avocados is delicious halved and served simply with dressing or stuffed and served hot or cold. To soften an underripe avocado, place it unpeeled in the oven and heat on high for 1 minute, or until slightly softened. Let it cool completely before using. The skin may brown or discolour slightly, but it will be perfectly fine underneath.

babaco A **fruit** of the papaya family grown commercially in New Zealand. Babaco has a thin, waxy, yellow, edible skin with yellow flesh and a white fibrous centre. It tastes of a combination of strawberries, pineapple and papaya. It must be eaten when ripe, so select fruits with shiny, yellow and undamaged skins. Wash and dry, and slice into rings or lengths, then cut into cubes.

baby food Baby food is specially prepared to be easily eaten and digested by infants. Commercially prepared baby food is available in cans and jars, with different particle sizes for different age groups. Strained baby food is suitable for 4–8 months old, small particle size for 8–12 months old and chewable for over 12 months. Canned and packaged baby food is ready for consumption and requires only warming to a comfortable temperature before use. Follow manufacturers' instructions on packs for heating times, and remember to remove metal lids from jars first. Milk can be reheated in plastic bottles or feeder jugs. Always test how hot the food is before serving, especially milk because 'hot spots' within the milk could cause scalding; shake the bottle and test it on the wrist first.

bacon Meat from the back and sides of a pig, which has been dried, salted or smoked. Smoking gives bacon its distinctive flavour, golden-brown rind and deep pink flesh. Unsmoked salt bacon is described as 'green'. Bacon is cut in to slices or rashers, the thicker slices are called steaks and large pieces called joints. Bacon rashers vary in thickness, as well as in sugar and fat content. To ensure that bacon cooks evenly, choose rashers of equal thickness and with a similar fat-to-lean ratio. Do not let bacon rashers overlap because they do not cook properly.

TO COOK: lay the rashers on a plate lined with white absorbent kitchen paper, cover with another sheet and cook on high, allowing 30–45 seconds for 1 rasher, $1-1\frac{1}{2}$ minutes for 2 rashers and $2-2\frac{1}{2}$ for 4 rashers. The timings will depend on the size and thickness of the rashers. If very crispy bacon is required, for salads or toppings, cook a further 30 seconds or so. Remove covering paper at once to prevent sticking.

To cook bacon steaks, snip into any fat at 2.5 cm (1 in) intervals. Place on a **bacon rack** and cover with absorbent paper. For 2, 75 g steaks, cook on high for 4 minutes, turning over halfway through cooking. Remove the paper to prevent it sticking, cover the steaks and **stand** for 2–3 minutes.

To cook bacon joints, soak in cold water for several hours to remove excess salt; drain and place inside a pierced **roasting bag** and stand in a **roasting dish**. Cook on high allowing 13–15 minutes for a 450 g joint, and 16–20 minutes for a 1 kg joint. Turn the joint round and over during cooking. Allow to stand for 10 minutes before serving. See also **gammon**.

bacon rack A specially designed plastic dish with ridges, that allows fat to run off, particularly when cooking bacon. See also **cookware**.

bacteria Microscopic organisms present in the body and in almost every form of food, which, if allowed to multiply, may cause **food poisoning**. Bacteria in food is destroyed by heat therefore it is important to follow cooking times in microwave recipes to ensure that the food is completely cooked.

bagel A ring of baked yeast dough with a chewy centre and a crusty outside. Bagels can be heated in the microwave, wrapped in kitchen paper, for a few seconds on high. Use damp kitchen paper to help crisp any stale bagels, and cook on high for 15 seconds.

baked bean A baked haricot bean canned in a tasty tomato sauce. Baked beans are a popular snack, commonly served on toast.

TO COOK: empty the contents of a 400 g can into a microwave dish, cover and reheat on high for 2–3 minutes until bubbling, stirring once or twice.

baked potato Probably one of the most popular foods prepared in the microwave, because, in small numbers, they are cooked in a fraction of the time it takes to bake them conventionally. The skins will not be crisp, but the flavour of the potato is very good. A wholesome meal can be made out of a baked **potato** by mixing the flesh with a tasty filling.

TO COOK: wash and dry the potatoes, and prick the skins with a fork or they will burst. Wrap them in absorbent paper and place on the floor of the cooker, and if cooking several, arrange them evenly spaced in a circle. Cook on high, for 1, 175 g potato allow 5 minutes, 2 potatoes, 6–8 minutes, 4, 10–12 minutes. Rearrange them once or twice during cooking, then **stand** for 5 minutes.

baking A method of cooking food, especially bread and **cakes**, in an oven without the addition of liquid. Baking cakes and **biscuits** in the microwave is very difficult and is rarely completely successful. Choose recipes that have been developed specifically for the microwave.

baking beans Ceramic baking beans, which look like small opaque marbles, are used instead of traditional baking beans when cooking pastry cases 'blind' in the microwave. Place a layer of greaseproof paper over the raw pastry case, spread a layer of beans onto the paper and leave them there for two thirds of the cooking time. Remove the beans and paper, and complete the cooking without them.

baking powder An alternative for yeast used as a raising agent in **baking** cakes and bread. This leavening agent can be bought or home-made from cream of tartar, bicarbonate of soda and salt. Be careful to use only the exact amount of baking powder stated in the recipe, because too much can spoil the texture of the food.

bamboo shoot The tender, cream-coloured young shoot of an edible bamboo plant. Bamboo shoots are usually sold in cans as whole shoots or slices. Once opened the shoots should be transferred to a non-metal container and stored in the refrigerator for up to a week, but change the water regularly. They are used mainly in Chinese cooking, traditionally in stir-fry dishes.

banana The yellow, crescent-shaped fruit of a variety of tropical and subtropical treelike plants. Choose firm, plump, bright yellow fruit that is undamaged. A green tip indicates an unripe banana, a completely yellow fruit is riper and one with brown specks is at prime ripeness. Do not store in the refrigerator

because the skins will turn black. Bananas may
be used in cakes, or baked, barbecued and in
drinks.

TO COOK: use firm bananas; peel and cut into
thick slices then place in a dish. Sprinkle over a
little lemon juice and 5 ml (1 tsp) of brown
sugar per banana, and add the zest of an orange
for a delicious flavour. Cover the dish and cook
on high allowing 2–3 minutes for 2 bananas
and 3–4 minutes for 4 bananas. Leave to **stand**
for 2 minutes.

barbecue sauce For foods that cannot be
cooked on a **browning dish**, brushing barbecue
sauce on meat or poultry during cooking will
add flavour and colour to the food. Barbecue
sauce, such as sweet and sour sauce, to accompany barbecue foods can also be prepared in
the microwave. See also **browning agent**.

barbecue seasoning A mixture of spices
that can be sprinkled onto foods, such as beefburgers, before cooking to add flavour and
colouring. See also **browning agent**.

barley See **pearl barley**.

barley water A soft drink made from **pearl
barley** boiled in water and flavoured with
orange or lemon juice.

TO MAKE: put 4 tbsp of pearl barley in a jug

with 600 ml of water, add orange or lemon rind and cook on high for 10 minutes. Strain and cool then sweeten with sugar or honey.

basil The aromatic leaves of a Eurasian plant, used as a **herb**. There are many varieties of basil, all with the same rich, peppery flavour. Basil goes particularly well with tomatoes and is often used in tomato-based dishes and the classic Italian sauce Pesto. Basil is excellent for seasoning soups, rice dishes and in salads.

basmati rice An aromatic, long, narrow-grained **rice**, most often used in Indian dishes.

bass Any of a variety of sea perches with firm, white flesh, and cooked whole or in fillets.
   TO COOK: wrap whole fish in greaseproof paper, and add seasoning as desired. Cook on high for 4–6 minutes per 450 g and **stand** for 3 minutes.

batter A mixture of flour, eggs and milk, commonly used to make pancakes and York-shire pudding. Batter mixtures cannot be cooked in the microwave.

bay The leaf of a Mediterranean laurel tree. Bay is usually included in a **bouquet garni** and may be used either dry or fresh. It is a good herb to use in casseroles, soups and stews and

17

to flavour milk to make sauces, such as bread sauce. Fresh bay leaves make an attractive garnish for patés and when serving cheeses. See also **herbs**.

bean Many pods and seeds have a dual role, first when they are young and fresh, and another after they have been dried, when they become known as **pulses**. When choosing pods select small, crisp and bright, fresh-looking varieties. See also **broad bean**; **French bean**; **runner bean**.

beansprout The sprout of a mung bean, which has a translucent white colour with a tapering root at one end, and a pale yellow pod at the other. When sprouted they are juicy and good in stir-fries and salads.

TO COOK: rinse 225 g of beansprouts under running water and put into a bowl. Cover the bowl and cook on high for 2 minutes, stirring once. Time carefully, they should be still quite crisp after cooking.

beef The meat of various bovine animals, particularly the cow. Beef can be cooked successfully in the microwave and is generally as tender and moist as conventionally cooked dishes. Choose evenly shaped cuts; roasts should have a regular diameter, meat for stews and casseroles should be of good quality and cut to a uniform size, and steaks should be of the same density throughout. However, tougher cuts that normally require long, slow conventional cooking to tenderize them should be avoided. To ensure even cooking, turn roasts and stir or rotate casseroles. Overcooking, especially on large rolled roasts, can be prevented by **shielding** ends with foil for part of the cooking time. Thinner ends of meat should always be shielded, as should bony portions. Small cuts cook well on high, but larger cuts are more tender when cooked at a lower power level.

Meat that will not brown during microwaving, such as a pot roast cooked in a **roasting bag**, can be first browned conventionally in a frying pan. **Browning agents** can also be used.

When choosing beef joints for cooking in the microwave, make sure that there is an even marbling of fat throughout for tender results. There are various ways to cook joints of beef in the microwave. Stand on a roasting rack over a shallow dish and cover with a slit roasting bag, tie the bag loosely and place in a dish, thereby preventing the meat from cooking in its own juices and becoming soggy.

TO COOK: joints on the bone, such as rib, should be cooked on high for the first 6–8 minutes then on medium power for 5–6 minutes per 450 g for rare meat, 6–7 minutes per 450 g for medium and 7–9 minutes for well done. Drain off any liquid halfway through cooking and tent with foil and **stand** for 15 minutes.

Boned and rolled joints, such as silverside, top-rump and topside, can be pot roasted with flavourings like onions and herbs added to 150–300 ml of stock. Cook covered for 6–8 minutes on high for a 1.4 kg joint then a further 40–45 minutes on medium. Turn the meat over halfway through cooking. Stand for 20 minutes. A joint of brisket is cooked in the same way, but it will need covering with 600 ml of boiling water or stock. To test whether the cooking is complete a microwave meat thermometer can be used: 55°C (130°F) for rare, 65°C (150°F) for medium and 70°C (160°F) for well done – all these temperatures will rise on standing (see also appendix VI).

To braise beef, using slices or small chunks of chuck steak, place 450 g of meat in a bowl and mix with sliced onions, cover and cook on high for 5 minutes. Add 25 g of flour and 300 g of boiling stock and seasonings. Cover and cook on high for 5 minutes and then on medium for 45 minutes. Stand for 10 minutes.

To cook minced beef put 450 g in a bowl, with 2–3 tbsp of water and cook covered on high for 7–8 minutes. Stir 2 or 3 times during cooking to break up lumps and ensure even cooking. Add any sauce ingredients, vegetables and herbs after halfway through cooking and add an extra 5 minutes.

beefburger A flat cake made of ground beef and seasonings, although other meats and poultry may also be cooked in the same way. The most widely available beefburgers are made from coarsely ground chuck steak and brisket. To improve their colour it is best to use a **browning dish** (pre-heated according to the manufacturer's instructions) or to brush them with a **browning agent**.

TO COOK: arrange the beefburgers in a single layer. For fresh burgers cook 2, 50 g burgers for 3–4 minutes and 4 for 5–6 minutes on high. For 2, 100 g (quarter-pounders) allow 4–5 minutes and 4, 6–7 minutes also on high. To make a cheeseburger lay a slice of cheese onto the burger for the last 20 seconds.

For frozen burgers arrange as before and cook 2, 50 g burgers for 4–5 minutes, 4 for 6–7 minutes, 2, 100 g for $8\frac{1}{2}$–$6\frac{1}{2}$ minutes and 4, 100 g for 7–8 minutes. Allow to **stand** for 2–3 minutes.

beetroot The dark purple root of a variety of beet plant. Cooked beetroot may be served in salads or made into a soup called borsch. Young cooked beetroots are also good served as a hot vegetable.

TO COOK: wash the beetroots and trim off the stalks. Prick the skins with a fork and place in a dish with 3 tbsp of water. Cover and cook on high allowing 9–12 minutes for 225 g of beetroot and 12–18 minutes for 450 g. **Stand** for 5 minutes, uncover and peel – the skins should just rub off when fully cooked.

beurre manié A smooth paste made from equal quantities of flour and butter. It is added to casseroles to thicken the liquid to make a sauce.

biscuit A small, flat, dry, sweet or plain-baked cake, based on cereals, but including a variety of different ingredients and flavourings. It is not easy to cook biscuits in the microwave. Results are not usually successful because it is difficult to achieve an evenly-shaped, crisp golden biscuit.

However, biscuits that may be cooked in a container, and cut into squares or bars after cooking do microwave well. Flapjacks, for example, contain a high proportion of fat and sugar and so may be prepared quite well in the microwave. Ready-made biscuits can be warmed in the microwave to 'freshen' them up. Wrap 2–4 biscuits in kitchen paper and heat on high for 30–40 seconds until the biscuits are warm.

blackberry The black or purple fruits of the bramble. Buy or pick whole, firm, deep-coloured blackberries and wash and hull them if necessary.

TO COOK: put 450 g of blackberries in a dish, sprinkle with 75 g of sugar and cover. Cook on high for 4–6 minutes, stir halfway through cooking; **stand** for 3 minutes. They are excellent in pies or sorbets.

blackcurrant The small black fruit of a temperate shrub. Choose firm, fully ripe fruit and remove the stems before cooking; this is easily done with bunches of currants by drawing the prongs of a fork down through the clusters.

TO COOK: put 450 g of blackcurrants in a dish with 2 tbsp of water and 100 g of sugar. Cover and cook on high for 5–6 minutes, stirring once. **Stand** for 3 minutes. Blackcurrants may be use to make pies, tarts, ice cream, sorbet and topping for cheesecake.

black-eyed bean A small, cream-coloured, kidney shaped bean with a distinctive black 'eye'. Black-eyed beans have a pleasant, slightly sweet flavour when cooked.

TO COOK: after soaking, put into a large dish and cover with fresh boiling water. Cover the dish and cook on high, ensuring that the beans are boiling hard for the first 10 minutes, and allow 20–30 minutes per 225 g of beans. Stir 2

or 3 times during cooking and then leave to
stand for 5–10 minutes. Cook for a further 5–10
minutes if still hard. See also **pulses**.

black kidney bean A shiny, black, kidney
shaped dried bean. Black kidney beans have a
pleasant flavour and smooth texture when
cooked. They are good in vegetable casseroles
and excellent in a mixed bean salad.

   TO COOK: soak the beans, then put them into a
large dish and cover with fresh boiling water.
Cover the dish and cook on high, ensuring that
the beans are boiling hard for the first 10
minutes, and allow 20–30 minutes for 225 g of
beans. Stir 2 or 3 times during cooking and then
leave to **stand** for 5–10 minutes. Cook for a
further 5–10 minutes if still hard. See also
pulses.

black pudding A mixture of pig's blood, pork
fat and cereals, put into a casing and simmered.
Black pudding can be bought in slices or in a
sausage shape. A **browning dish** may be used to
cook the slices (pre-heat the dish according to
the manufacturer's instructions).

   TO COOK: arrange in a single layer on kitchen
paper and turn over and rearrange during
cooking. Microwave on high, allowing $3–3\frac{1}{2}$
minutes for 225 g of black pudding and 4–5
minutes for 450 g.

blanching A process of immersing fruit and vegetables briefly into boiling water to stop enzyme activity, which would otherwise continue (even at freezer temperature) causing loss of flavour, colour and texture. Blanching is also used to pre-cook and tenderize food as well as to loosen skins. A microwave is particularly useful when blanching fruit and vegetables for the freezer.

Before blanching, clean, trim and slice the vegetables to a uniform size. To blanch 450 g of vegetables, place in a casserole or bowl with 150 ml ($\frac{1}{4}$ pint) of water. Cover and cook on high for approximately 3–5 minutes, depending on variety. Stir once halfway through the blanching time. Drain then plunge into iced water. Once chilled, drain well and pack for the freezer.

bloater (also called **buckling**) An inshore herring that is usually lightly salted and then smoked. Bloater can be eaten cold, with a salad, or served hot.

TO COOK: place in a buttered dish and also dot with butter. Cover the dish and cook 1 bloater on high for 3–4 minutes, turning over halfway through cooking. **Stand** for 2 minutes.

blueberry A small blue-black berry of a North American shrub, with an attractive bloom on its skin. Blueberries can be used uncooked in pies and muffins, and are excellent in a pie or as a sorbet. When preparing fresh blueberries for cooking first remove any stalks and leaves.

TO COOK: put 450 g of blueberries in a dish and sprinkle with 75 g of sugar. Cover the dish and cook on high for 4–6 minutes, stirring halfway through cooking. **Stand** for 3 minutes.

bockwurst A white sausage made from veal and pork. Always pierce its skin before cooking to prevent it from bursting.
TO COOK: place into a dish and cook 1 sausage on high for 45 seconds, 2 for 1 minute and 4 for 1½–2 minutes.

boiling As in conventional cooking boiling is the method of cooking food in boiling liquid. The foods that are usually cooked in this way are vegetables, pasta and rice. However, because microwave cooking is a naturally moist form of cooking, less liquid is usually needed than in conventional boiling.

boiling bags See **roasting bags**.

borlotti bean (also called **rose coco bean**) A beige or pale brown bean speckled with burgundy markings. Borlotti beans may be used in salads, soups, stews and casseroles. They are the most popular dried bean in Italy.

26

TO COOK: after soaking, rinse the beans and place them in a large dish, then cover with fresh, boiling water. Cover the dish and cook on high, ensuring that the beans are boiling hard for the first 10 minutes, allowing 20–30 minutes for 225 g of beans. Stir 2 or 3 times during cooking and then leave to **stand** for 5–10 minutes. Cook for a further 5–10 minutes if still hard. See also **pulses**.

bouquet garni A selection of **herbs**, usually comprising of a sprig of parsley, thyme and a bay leaf, tied together in a bundle and used to flavour stocks, soups and stews. To dry a bouquet garni in the microwave, place between sheets of kitchen paper and cook on high for 25 seconds.

brain The brain of a calf or lamb eaten as **offal**. Brains are always sold in sets and provide a very soft, pale meat. Calf brain has a more delicate flavour than lamb. To improve its appearance, the fine membrane that covers the brain can be removed by soaking in cold water for 30 minutes and carefully pulling the membrane away.

TO COOK: place 450 g of brain in a bowl and cover with stock. Cook on high for 6–8 minutes, then on medium for 10–12 minutes. Drain and slice, coat with eggs and breadcrumbs and cook on high in a **browning dish** –

pre-heated for 5 minutes. Then add 25 g of butter, press the slices down and cook for a further 3–8 minutes, turning the slices once; serve at once.

braising A method of cooking in which the food, usually meat, is lightly fried and then allowed to simmer slowly in a small amount of liquid. Food braised in the microwave does not need to be fried first, because it will not take as long as conventional cooking. For the best results, select a more tender cut of good quality meat or choose poultry and vegetables that do not need a long cooking time. See also **beef**; **chicken**; **pork**.

bramble See **blackberry**.

bratwurst A pale sausage made from finely ground pork, veal, chopped onion and seasonings. It is commonly served with potato salad and sauerkraut.

TO COOK: first pre-heat a **browning dish** if being used. Cook 225 g of sausages on high for 4–5 minutes and 450 g for 6–7 minutes, turning them over and rearranging several times during cooking.

brazil nut The crescent-shaped **nut** of a tropical South American tree, with a woody, brown shell and an off-white kernel. Brazil nuts are best bought in the autumn and winter, and have a better flavour if bought in their shells. Shelled nuts may be served with fruit and cheese, but when blanched and chopped they may be used in cakes, biscuits, nut cutlets, stuffings and salads.

bread A food made from dough. Baking bread in a microwave does not compare very well to a conventionally baked loaf. The texture, taste and appearance of the bread is not as good. However, a microwave can be used successfully for 'proving' bread dough. Place 675 g of dough in an oiled polythene bag and cook on low for 4 minutes. Teabreads and scones are suitable for microwaving, although they will have a pale appearance. When cooking a teabread in the microwave, stand it on a trivet or rack and rotate the dish during cooking.

Most breads reheat successfully in the microwave. Wrap the bread in kitchen paper to absorb moisture, and reheat on high for 1 minute just before serving. To freshen slightly stale bread, heat on high for about 15 seconds. Use the microwave for **defrosting** and warming frozen bread, baking individual slices or single items from the freezer and defrosting them as needed. Allow 20–30 seconds for 1 slice of bread on the defrost setting. See also **breadcrumbs**.

breadcrumbs To make dry breadcrumbs heat a slice of bread for 2–3 minutes on high and leave to cool. When cold it will become crisp and can be crushed with a rolling pin or in a blender. Breadcrumbs, seasoned or unseasoned, may be used on top of uncovered food or casseroles to improve their appearance.

bread sauce Traditionally English bread sauce is used to accompany roast chicken, turkey and game birds.

TO MAKE: put 250 ml of milk into a jug with $\frac{1}{2}$ a sliced onion, 2 cloves, 1 bay leaf, a few peppercorns and cook on high for 3–4 minutes until the milk is scalded. Allow to cool. Strain into a bowl and then stir in 25 g of fresh breadcrumbs. Return the sauce to the microwave and cook for 3–4 minutes, or until the sauce has thickened, stirring every minute. Then mix in 25 g of butter and season to taste before serving.

bream A round red and silver **fish** with white, mild-tasting flesh. Nearly always sold whole it will need to be scaled, gutted and trimmed of its fins before cooking.

TO COOK: bream is best baked whole. Score the fish and place it in a dish with a little olive oil and lemon juice, add herbs and marinate for 1 hour. Cover and cook on high for 4–6 minutes per 450 g. **Stand** for 5 minutes.

brill A flatfish with a firm texture, similar to turbot. It is often too big to cook whole, so it is cut into fillets and steaks.

TO COOK: place the **fish** in a greased dish, season, cover and then cook on high for 4–6 minutes per 450 g, turning halfway through cooking. **Stand** for 5 minutes.

brisket The undersection of the fore-quarter and ribs of **beef**. Brisket is usually bought as a piece, which has been boned and rolled. It is a tougher than most cuts of meat, therefore it is not suitable for roasting in a microwave.

broad bean The pale green seed of a Eurasian bean plant. If the broad bean is very young the pod is edible and older broad bean seeds can be made into a good soup.

TO COOK: put 225 g of podded beans into a dish with 3 tbsp of water, cover and cook on high for 5–6 minutes, stirring halfway. Dot with butter and **stand** for 5 minutes.

broccoli (also called **calabrese**) The flower-head of a variety of cabbage. Select fresh-coloured, compact heads with tender stalks, and avoid yellow heads or any beginning to flower. Broccoli is available throughout the year.

TO COOK: cut the broccoli florets off the stalks into equal-sized pieces. Wash thoroughly, place them into a dish with the heads towards the centre and add 2 tbsp of water. Cover the dish and cook 225 g on high for 4–5 minutes, rearranging halfway through cooking. **Stand** for 2 minutes and then drain and season.

browning agent   Most food is cooked in the microwave so quickly that its surfaces are not exposed to heat changes, so it does not dry out, crisp and brown as it would in a conventional oven. Some foods with a good fat covering, such as bacon joints, will brown because the fat rises to the surface. Some foods can be cooked on a **browning dish** to improve their appearance, but there is also a wide range of ingredients that can enhance the look of microwaved food.

Dark sauces, such as soy, teriyaki, diluted gravy browning, barbecue and Worcestershire sauce, can all be brushed on to food, as can a glaze of marmalade. Coating the food with spice and herb mixtures, with or without breadcrumbs, may be used. Toasted chopped nuts and brown sugar also help to improve the look of pale microwaved food. Commercially prepared microwave browning agents are also available, which are generally used on meat and poultry before cooking.

browning dish   The only dish that can be put into the microwave when empty. A browning dish has a special coating on its base that absorbs microwave energy and becomes very hot, usually there is also a well around the edge to catch drippings. When using a browning dish it must always be pre-heated for at least 5 minutes on high before use. Fat and oil is quickly swirled on and then the food is pressed on to the hot surface, then turned over and browned on the other side. There is no need to pre-heat the dish to cook the second side, however, the dish must be pre-heated between batches of food. Microwave cooking can then continue in the same dish, with the microwaves being attracted to the food rather than the coating of the dish. Some browning dishes have a non-stick surface, which means that the dish does not need to be coated with fat before cooking.

browning grill This is an element fitted into the roof of the microwave oven cavity. Although it is less powerful than a conventional grill it can be used for browning foods before or after cooking. When using this facility care must be taken to use a container made from a suitable material, such as ceramic or glass, because plastic will melt.

brown sugar Unrefined or partially refined sugar, produced only from cane sugar. Brown sugar contains some molasses, which give it its characteristic colour and flavour. Brown sugar may be light or dark and is most often used in baking.

Brussels sprout The small bud of a variety of cabbage. Choose fresh, tightly-closed green sprouts and all roughly the same size, and avoid any that are yellowing or wilted. Trim off any damaged leaves and wash thoroughly.

TO COOK: put 450 g of sprouts in a dish with 6 tbsp of water. Cover the dish and cook on high for 7–8 minutes, stirring once or twice during cooking. **Stand** for 2 minutes. Once cooked the sprouts should be firm, but tender.

buckling See **bloater**.

buckwheat An annual plant that produces triangular seeds. Buckwheat is not a cereal, but it can be used in much the same way as cereal grains. It can be bought as grains, roasted or unroasted, and as a flour. Roasted buckwheat is the basis of a dish called Kasha, or it can be cooked and used instead of rice. Buckwheat flour is also used to make blini (a type of pancake).

TO COOK: put 225 g of buckwheat into a bowl and cover with 900 ml of boiling water. Microwave on high for 8–10 minutes or until the grains are tender. **Stand** for 5 minutes, then drain off any excess water and season to taste.

bulgar (also called **cracked wheat**) A form of wheat in which the wholewheat grains are steamed until partly cooked, then dried thoroughly and cracked or crushed in coarse or fine grades. Bulgar is used in many Middle Eastern dishes and is particularly delicious in pilafs.

TO COOK: place 100 g of bulgar in a bowl, pour in 300 ml of boiling water and stir well. Cover the bowl and cook on high for 2–3 minutes. Allow to **stand** for 5 minutes, then drain, fork through and season well.

butter A fatty whitish-yellow paste made from churning the cream of cows' milk. To soften butter in the microwave, wrap 100 g in greaseproof paper, place on a plate and heat on low or the defrost setting for 30–40 seconds until spreadable. To clarify butter put 100 g of cubed butter into a glass measuring jug, heat on high for $1\frac{1}{2}$–2 minutes until melted, and then skim the foam from the top.

butter bean A dried variety of lima bean, which is flat and kidney shaped. Butter beans are a tasty bean with a mealy texture that absorbs other flavours well.

TO COOK: after soaking put the beans into a large dish and cover with fresh boiling water. Cover the dish and cook 225 g on high for 20–30 minutes, ensuring that the beans are boiling hard for the first 10 minutes. Stir 2 or 3

35

times during cooking and then leave to **stand** for 5–10 minutes. Cook for a further 5–10 minutes if still hard. See also **pulses**.

buttermilk A cultured milk product made from pasteurized skimmed milk. Buttermilk is low in fat, mildly acidic, with a creamy taste and thick consistency. It can be used for making milkshakes, but it may also be used in baking, e.g. breads, cakes or scones.

butternut squash A cream-coloured **squash**, which is often available in the autumn. Wash the **fruit** thoroughly, cut in half, remove the seeds and place, cut-side down, in a dish.

TO COOK: cover the dish and cook 450 g on high for 7–8 minutes. Cooked butternut squash can be added to soups, purées and desserts. When mature it can also be used to make jams, preserves and pickles.

button onion A small onion about 1 cm in diameter, usually with papery, brown skins, but occasionally white. Button onions are a fiddle to peel so **blanch** them for 1–2 minutes to loosen the skins so that they can be easily removed. Serve them as a vegetable on their own or add to stews and casseroles.

cabbage   The large leafy bud of a variety of European plant. At least one variety of cabbage or another is available all year, but most cabbages are at their best in winter. Varieties to choose from include spring greens, January King, roundhead cabbage, savoy, white Dutch cabbage and red cabbage. Before cooking remove any loose or damaged leaves, wash thoroughly in cold water and then shred.

TO COOK: place the cabbage in a dish with 2 tbsp of water. Cover the dish and cook 225 g on high for 2–4 minutes and 5–7 minutes for 450 g of cabbage. Stir once during cooking and then allow to **stand** for 2 minutes. Drain, season and serve. When cooking red cabbage increase the cooking time by about 2 minutes. Red cabbage may also be braised in stock with apples and onions.

cake   Microwaved cakes are light textured and moist, and can be prepared in a fraction of the time it takes to conventionally bake them. However, some types of cake made in a microwave, for example a plain sponge, will lack a golden colour. So it is best to choose recipes that are naturally moist with ingredients that provide a good rich colour, such as chocolate or gingerbread. Because very moist cake mixtures work best it helps to add an extra egg or 15–30 ml of water or milk to give a softer consistency. If using dried fruit in the mixture, plump it up and soften it in water or fruit juice on high for three minutes.

Cakes rise spectacularly in the microwave, so make sure that the container used is deep enough to allow for the extra rising otherwise the mixture will spill over. Do not fill the dish more than half-full with mixture. Use special microwave cake dishes, which are flexible, because this helps when turning the cake out. The types of containers that produce the best cakes are **ring moulds** or moulds with rounded edges.

Stand the cake dish on a trivet or rack, and to ensure that it is evenly cooked rotate the dish halfway through cooking. To test if a cake is done pierce it with a skewer halfway between the edge and the centre. If the skewer comes out clean the cake is ready even if the surface still appears moist and sticky. Any such moist spots will dry out during the **standing time**. Never cover cakes with clingfilm because the steam produced during cooking must be able to escape.

calabrese See **broccoli**.

candied fruit Whole or sections of fruit that are almost entirely dehydrated and then saturated with sugar by processing in a syrup. Fruits, such as mixed peel and glacé cherries, are commonly used as an ingredient in cakes, biscuits, desserts or ice cream. Candied fruit can be softened and flavoured with a liqueur in the microwave. Put 60 ml of liqueur into a bowl and heat on high for 30 seconds. Add 150 g of candied and glacé fruit. Stir to mix and then heat on high for 2 minutes, and allow to **stand** until the liquid is absorbed.

cannelloni Large tubes of **pasta**, approximately 10 cm long, that may be ridged or plain. Once boiled and softened cannelloni can be stuffed, covered in a sauce and reheated.

TO COOK: pour enough boiling water into a dish to immerse the pasta. Add 1 tbsp of oil and a little salt. Cook with the dish uncovered, allowing 6–8 minutes for 225 g of dried pasta. **Stand** for 5 minutes and then drain. Fresh pasta takes less time to cook, so heat on high for 1–2 minutes.

cape gooseberry A small, golden fruit with a sharp flavour from South Africa. Choose firm, large, evenly coloured berries with a fragrant smell. Cape gooseberries may be used in fresh fruit salad or in ice cream, sorbet or jam.

caper The flower buds of a spiny, trailing Mediterranean shrub. Capers are usually available preserved pickled and are used in salads, sauces, especially black butter sauce, and as a garnish.

capon A castrated young cockerel. Capons are usually larger than most chickens, ranging in weight from 2.7 kg to 4.5 kg. They are prized for their tenderness and have a large proportion of white meat compared to dark meat.

TO COOK: cover the wings, leg tips and the breastbone with smooth pieces of **foil** to prevent over-cooking. Put the bird in to a pierced **roasting bag** and place it breast-side down in a **roasting dish**. Cook on medium allowing 7–9 minutes per 450 g and turn over halfway through cooking. If using a thermometer, remove the capon when it reads 82–85°C. Then allow it to **stand** for 15 minutes, during which time the temperature will rise to 85–87°C. During standing time always **tent** a capon with foil to keep it warm. To test if the bird is done, pierce the thickest part of the thigh with a skewer and the juices should run clear without a trace of pink.

To cook capon portions, arrange the portions carefully to ensure that they are all evenly cooked. Place the meatier pieces towards the edge of the dish and bonier parts towards the centre. Over-cooking of boneless capon breasts can be prevented by tucking the thinner ends underneath. As well as using browning agents, capon portions can also be cooked in a **browning dish**. Alternatively, capon pieces cooked in the microwave can be placed under a grill to crisp and brown. When cooking in a sauce, remove the skin and any fat first otherwise, the sauce will be greasy. By removing the skin it also helps the flavourings to penetrate the flesh better. Cook 2, 225 g capon portions on high for 6–8 minutes and 2, 175 g skinned and boned capon breasts for 5–6 minutes. Allow to stand for 5 minutes. See also **chicken**; **poussin**.

capsicum Any of several varieties of tropical American plants with seeds used to make pepper. With their bright colours and fresh flavour, sweet peppers are useful both raw in salads and cooked in casseroles, stir-fries and vegetable mixtures. Cored and de-seeded peppers make perfect containers for a stuffing. Choose peppers with firm, glossy skins.

TO COOK: remove the core and seeds, cut into rings, slices or halves. Cook 225 g of peppers covered in 1 tbsp of water or oil for 2–3 minutes. See **cayenne pepper**; **chilli**; **peppers**.

caramel A mixture of sugar and water that is cooked until it turns brown. Caramel can vary in colour from pale gold to very dark brown. Its texture can also vary, from soft and pliable to the hard-crack stage used in nut brittles. Making caramel in the microwave is quick, safe and easier than in a conventional oven.

TO COOK: use a glass jug or bowl so that the colour of the caramel can be seen. The top of the jug or bowl must be tightly covered (e.g.

with **clingfilm**), so that the steam produced during the cooking can condense and run back down into the mixture. This helps to make sure that the mixture is cooked evenly. It is best not to stir because this will cloud the caramel.

The caramel continues to cook after it has been removed from the oven, so remove it from the oven the moment it turns the colour desired. Remove the covering carefully because the steam will be very hot. Then make the caramel according to the recipe used.

caraway seed A tiny crescent-shaped, brown-black **seed** with a strong aromatic flavour. Caraway seeds are traditionally used in English seed cake and Hungarian goulash.

cardamon, cardamom or **cardamum** The seed of a tropical Asian plant used as a **spice**. Cardamon seeds have a pungent, spicy, sweet flavour and a eucalyptus-like aroma. Remove the seeds from the pods and crush them to release their flavour. Cardamon is used extensively in Indian food and certain Danish pastries.

care of the microwave It is best to place the oven in a non-confined, well ventilated space and away from any source of heat or hot air. Always unplug the oven before moving it and never move the oven when in use. The oven should not be operated when empty because this could damage the unit. It is a good idea to leave a cup of water in the oven, when not being used for cooking, to prevent this from happening by mistake. Never use the oven cavity as a storage cupboard or to dry or heat clothes, papers or any items other than food. Never put undue strain on the door by hanging items from it. Never attempt to close the oven door when there is an object between it and the oven, or the door seal may become damaged. See also **cleaning a microwave oven**; **safety of a microwave oven**.

carob A cocoa substitute obtained from grinding the pod of a variety of evergreen Mediterranean tree. Carob looks and tastes similar to cocoa and is a little sweeter. Use it to darken microwave-baked cakes, biscuits, desserts, confectionery and milk drinks.

carp A large freshwater fish. Carp has a tendency to taste muddy, but this can be eliminated by soaking it well before cooking. Wash the fish in a mild vinegar-water solution for 2–3 hours.

TO COOK: score along the sides of the fish, place it in a greased dish and dot with butter. Cover the dish, cook on high, allowing 4–6 minutes per 450 g, and turn over halfway through cooking. **Stand** for 5 minutes.

carrot A crisp root vegetable with orange flesh. Carrots are available all year, but are best in the spring. Choose firm, smooth, well-shaped, bright orange carrots, and avoid any with cracks or soft, wet areas. Wash them in cold water, trim off the tops and tails, and cook with the skin on or peel very thinly. Leave baby carrots whole, but cut larger ones into **julienne** strips or slice.

TO COOK: place the prepared carrots in a dish with 3 tbsp of water. Cover the dish and cook 225 g on high for 5–6 minutes and 450 g for 6–8 minutes. Stir during cooking and then allow to **stand** for 2–3 minutes.

cashew nut The kidney shaped **nut** of a tropical South American tree, used whole for snacks, or chopped and added to salads, nut cutlets or stuffings.

cassava A long brown tuber, which when peeled reveals a fibrous white flesh. Cassava in its dry powdered form is often used as a thickener for curry sauces and stewed dishes. See also **tapioca**.

casserole Any food cooked and served in a covered dish. Meat can be stewed (casseroled) in the microwave, provided that the leaner, tender cuts of meat like **lamb**, **veal** and **pork** are used. Tougher cuts give a disappointing result because the flavours do not develop and mingle in the same way as in slow conventional cooking. The meat fibres do not have enough time to break down and become tender.

catalytic lining A **combination oven** is less easy to clean than a standard microwave because the food has a tendency to bake on. However, the catalytic lining has a 'stay clean' property to help keep the oven clean. Fat splashed onto the lining is absorbed and burnt off during cooking. The lining is effective at medium and high temperatures.

cauliflower The tightly packed, white flower of a variety of cabbage. Cauliflower is available all year, but most seasonal in winter. Choose a cauliflower with a white or creamy head, tightly packed flower buds (known as 'curd') and surrounded by fresh green leaves. Wash thoroughly and break into even-sized florets.

TO COOK: place in a dish and add 2–3 tbsp of water. Cover the dish and cook on high, allowing 4–5 minutes for 225 g and 6–8 minutes for 450 g. Stir during cooking and then allow to **stand** for 2–3 minutes.

cayenne pepper A particularly hot and pungent form of pepper, typically bright orange-red, made from the ground seeds and pods of a variety of capsicum. Useful for giving a 'kick' to bland dishes.

celeriac The large bulbous root of a variety of celery, with brown skin and white flesh. Celeriac has a sweet nutty flavour and is good both raw and cooked.

TO COOK: peel carefully and cut into slices or **julienne** strips. Put the strips into a dish and add 3 tbsp of water. Cover the dish and cook 225 g of celeriac on high for 5–7 minutes and 450 g for 8–10 minutes, stirring during cooking. Then drain well and toss in lemon juice.

To blanch celeriac for salads, cook for half the length of time. Then drain, cool and serve tossed in a mayonnaise or oil-based dressing.

celery The crisp white or green stalks of Eurasian shrub. Celery may be used raw in salad and is excellent in soups, casseroles, and stir-fries. Choose celery that is firm and crisp, with pale green straight leaves. Trim the root and break off the green leaves, pulling any strings away with them.

TO COOK: cut the stalks into 5 cm lengths, put them into a dish and add 4 tbsp of water. Cover the dish and cook 450 g of celery on high for 6–7 minutes, stirring halfway through cooking. Then **stand** for 3 minutes, drain and serve.

chapatti A flat disc of unleavened bread, made from milled wheat flour called *atta*. Buy chapatti fresh from supermarkets or Indian restaurants and eat on the same day. They are eaten warm often with Indian vegetable curry and rice. To warm in the microwave, wrap each chapatti in kitchen paper and heat on high for 1 minute per chapatti.

chayote The pear-shaped, green fruit of a tropical American vine eaten as a vegetable. Choose firm, small chayotes without any brown spots. They are often stuffed with savoury mixtures and can be used in chutney. To prepare for eating as a vegetable, cut them into quarter segments, slice off the peel and remove the seed, then cut into chunks.

TO COOK: place 225 g of prepared chayote into a dish with 2 tbsp of water. Cover the dish and cook on high for 4–5 minutes, stirring once. Drain and serve with a sauce.

cheese A dairy product made from the curd of milk separated from the whey, treated with rennet, allowed to clot and (with some varieties) to mature and ferment. Cheese needs to be gently cooked to avoid becoming tough and stringy. Full power can be used for melting cheese, but care must be taken not to overcook, so medium and lower power may give a better result. When making a cheese sauce, grate the cheese and add to a hot mixture to ensure that it melts and blends evenly. See also **cream cheese**.

cheesecake   Any of a variety of rich tarts on a biscuit base and made with either cream cheese, curd cheese, sieved cottage cheese or a combination of these varieties. Either cook cheesecake in the dish it is to be served, or cook the filling in a microwave dish and add the biscuit base towards the end of cooking time, then invert onto a plate. Cooked cheesecake can be topped with fresh berries, soured cream or canned pie filling.

cherimoya   See **custard apple**.

cherry   The small, round, red, purple or black fruit of the cherry tree, with sweet, juicy reddish flesh and a small hard stone. Most cherries are eaten fresh, some less sweet varieties are cooked and used in pies.

TO COOK: remove stones if preferred, put 450 g of cherries in a dish with 50–100 g of sugar and cover. Cook on high for 3–4 minutes, **stand** for 3 minutes.

chervil   A delicate aniseed-flavoured **herb**, which can be used in egg dishes, salads, and with poultry and fish. To dry chervil, place it between two sheets of kitchen paper and cook on high for 25 seconds.

chestnut   The nut of a variety of chestnut tree, which has a smooth, tough brown skin and wrinkled-looking yellowish flesh. Chestnuts are available during the autumn and winter, and it is best to buy chestnuts that are heavy for their size with undamaged shells. Raw chestnuts are not edible.

TO COOK: make horizontal cuts through the shells of 150 g of chestnuts, then put them into a jug with 250 ml of water. Cover the jug and heat on high for 3–4 minutes until boiling, then cook for a further minute. **Stand** for 5–10 minutes before peeling and re-boil any still not open.

chicken A domestic fowl and its meat. Chicken cooked in the microwave has moist flesh and succulent flavour, but the skin remains soft and pale. To make it as appetizing as possible, a whole chicken should be brushed with a **browning agent** or sauce to enhance its appearance. A whole bird will require **shielding** and turning halfway through cooking. Stuffing the cavity can insulate the bird and cooking the bird thoroughly can result in overcooking. It is best to put the stuffing in the neck end of the bird under the skin. Alternatively, cook and serve the stuffing separately. Other ingredients, such as onion, herbs and apple, may be loosely placed in the cavity.

To ensure an accurate reading when using a temperature probe make sure that the bird weighs at least 1.5 kg. Plain microwaved chicken is ideal for use in a main course salad and other cold dishes.

TO COOK: cover the wings, leg tips and the breastbone with smooth pieces of **foil** to prevent over-cooking. Put the bird in to a pierced **roasting bag** and place it breast-side down in a **roasting dish**. Cook on medium allowing 7–9 minutes per 450 g and turn over halfway through cooking. If using a thermometer, remove the chicken when it reads 80°C (175°F). Then allow it to **stand** for 15 minutes, during which time the temperature will rise to 85°C (185°F). During standing time always **tent** a chicken with foil to keep it warm. To test if the chicken is done, pierce the thickest part of the thigh with a skewer and the juices should run clear without a trace of pink.

To cook chicken portions, arrange the portions carefully to ensure that they are all evenly cooked. Place the meatier pieces towards the edge of the dish and bonier parts towards the centre. Over-cooking of boneless chicken breasts can be prevented by tucking the thinner ends underneath. As well as using browning agents, chicken portions can also be cooked in a **browning dish**. Alternatively, chicken pieces cooked in the microwave can be placed under a grill to crisp and brown. When cooking in a sauce, remove the skin and any fat first otherwise the sauce will be greasy. By removing the skin it also helps the flavourings to penetrate the flesh better. Cook 2, 225 g chicken portions on high for 6–8 minutes and 2, 175 g skinned and boned chicken breasts, 5–6 minutes. Allow to stand for 5 minutes. See also **capon; poussin**.

chicken liver　Can be cooked in the microwave and served with a sauce, a salad or made into paté. Care must be taken not to overcook chicken livers because they will quickly toughen. Trim, halve and wash the livers and pat dry on absorbent kitchen paper. Then prick them with a cocktail stick to prevent them from bursting during cooking.

TO COOK: put 25 g of butter in a dish and melt it by heating on high for 45 seconds. Add 225 g of chicken livers, cover and cook on high for 2–3 minutes, stirring once during cooking. **Stand** for 2 minutes.

chicken stock　This can be prepared easily in the microwave. Place the chicken carcass into a large bowl with a chopped leek, carrot and celery stick, season with a bouquet garni and add 1 litre of water. Cook on high for 20 minutes and allow to **stand** for 5 minutes, then strain the stock discarding the bones and vegetables.

chickpea　The round, beige coloured, dried fruit of a leguminous plant. Cooked chickpeas have a nutty flavour with a mealy texture. They are traditionally used in Indian dishes, soups, stews, casseroles, salads, vegetarian burgers and as purée, for example in Middle Eastern hummus.

TO COOK: first soak the chickpeas, then rinse and put them into a large dish, and immerse them in fresh, boiling water. Cover the dish and cook 225 g of chickpeas on high for 45–50 minutes, ensuring that the beans are boiling hard for the first 10 minutes, stirring 2 or 3 times during cooking. Leave to **stand** for 5–10 minutes. Cook a further 5–10 minutes if still hard. See also **pulses**.

chicory The green-white, tightly wrapped leaves of a blue-flowered plant, eaten as a vegetable. Chicory has a crisp and slightly bitter taste and is often added to salads, but it is also good braised. Choose fresh-coloured, crisp, tender-leaved shoots.

TO COOK: trim the base of each head and wash thoroughly. Then slice, lengthways, into two and arrange in a dish with the narrow parts to the centre. Add 1 tbsp of lemon juice and 1 tbsp of water. Cover the dish and cook 4 heads on high for 5–6 minutes, rearranging halfway through cooking. **Stand** for 3 minutes.

children using microwave Cooking in the microwave is the easiest and safest way for children to prepare food. Supervision will be needed for younger children and particular guidelines explained to all ages to prevent accidents or damage to the machine. Remind children always to read the recipe they are using and make sure they understand it and have all the necessary ingredients and cookware. Also make sure that oven gloves are used for handling hot dishes. See also **care of the microwave**; **safety of the microwave**.

chilli The red or green and red tapering pod of a tropical variety of **capsicum**. Chillies vary in hotness, usually the smaller the chilli the hotter it is. Care should be taken when handling fresh chillies, because they can cause a burning irritation to the skin and eyes.

chilli powder A powder made from the dried fruit of a hot, spicy pepper. The pungency of ground chillies varies from mild to very hot depending on the blend. Chilli powder is used in chilli con carne and other Mexican dishes. Like cayenne pepper, it can be used to give a 'kick' to mild dishes.

china Sturdy porcelain and china without any metal decoration or trim can be used successfully in the microwave. They can also make attractive oven-to-table containers, especially ramekin and gratin dishes and single plates when cooking or reheating for one. See also **cookware**.

Chinese cabbage See **Chinese leaf**.

Chinese gooseberry See **kiwi fruit**.

Chinese leaf (also called **Chinese cabbage**) A variety of cabbage with a tall, tightly packed bud of wrinkled green leaves on crisp, white stems. Select a fresh, crisp head with unmarked stems. Chinese leaves are good in salads or stir-fries.

TO COOK: trim the stalk and shred the leaves. Place in a dish and add 2 tbsp of water. Cover the dish and cook on high allowing 2–4 minutes for 225 g and 5–6 minutes for 450 g. Leave to **stand** for 2 minutes.

chip A strip of deep-fried potato. Potatoes cannot be fried in the microwave, and deep frying of any food must never be attempted in the microwave. However, frozen oven-ready chips can be cooked in the microwave, but only on a **browning dish**. Pre-heat the dish on high for 5 minutes or according to manufacturer's instructions.

TO COOK: place on a hot browning dish, cook 225 g for $3\frac{1}{2}$–4 minutes and stir the chips once or twice during cooking. Or cook in the packaging according to the manufacturer's instructions.

chipolata A small pork or pork and beef sausage about half the size of a standard sausage. Prick the sausage before cooking to prevent it from bursting.

TO COOK: pre-heat a **browning dish**, add 225 g of sausages and cook on high for 3–4 minutes, turning halfway and rearranging.

chive The thin tubular leaves of a Eurasian plant with a mild onion flavour. Chives are used as a **herb** in many dishes, such as salads, egg dishes, soups and for garnishing.

chocolate A hard, dark brown paste made from ground, roasted cocoa seeds, and usually sweetened and flavoured. Chocolate is used extensively in sweet dishes, to add colour and flavour. Biscuits, cakes, desserts, sauces and handmade sweets are all popular ways of cooking with chocolate. It can also be used for decoration either grated, chopped or curled, or melted and made into shapes.

Chocolate melts perfectly in the microwave. Place 25 g in a small bowl and heat uncovered on high for $1-1\frac{1}{2}$ minutes until just shiny. It will retain its shape until stirred. Remove from the oven and stir until completely melted and smooth. Do not overcook chocolate because it becomes thick, grainy, dull and difficult to handle.

choux pastry A very light pastry made with eggs. Choux pastry is used for making eclairs and choux buns. It cannot be cooked in the microwave because it needs dry heat to crisp and puff it up.

Christmas pudding A rich fruit pudding, traditionally steamed or boiled for many hours. Microwaving this type of pudding is a great time-saver. Because the flavours have less time to develop during cooking, the raw mixture should be left to stand overnight according to the recipe and spooned into a greased 1.2 litre pudding basin.

TO COOK: place a plate over the basin and cook on medium for 25 minutes. Leave the basin covered and allow to **stand** for 5 minutes before turning the pudding out. To cook a bought Christmas pudding, remove it from the container, cover with a bowl and cook on medium for 5 minutes.

To reheat, cut the pudding into portions and arrange the portions, spaced apart, on a serving plate. Put a glass of water in the centre of the plate, this produces steam which keeps the pudding moist. Cover the plate with a large, upturned bowl and cook on high for 2–3 minutes. Individual portions can be reheated uncovered on a plate on high for 1–2 minutes.

chunk An irregular shaped piece of food, larger than cubes and thicker than slices.

chutney A pickle made from fruit, vegetables, spices, vinegar, sugar and salt. The microwave is ideal for making small, quantities of chutney and relishes. The ingredients are unlikely to burn because there is no direct heat to the bowl. Ingredients need to be finely chopped or minced then cooked with the sugar, vinegar and flavouring ingredients to a thick sauce with no surplus liquid. Pour into hot, sterilized jars and cover with acid-proof lids. Label them and store in a cool dark place. See also **preserves**.

cinnamon A fragrant, yellow-brown bark of a tropical tree, which is ground and used as a **spice** in both sweet and savoury dishes. Ground cinnamon is a traditional ingredient in mixed spice and curry powder.

citrus fruit The **fruits** of certain varieties of tropical and subtropical trees, characterized by a waxy rind and flesh in crescent-shaped segments. To squeeze citrus fruit more easily, place the fruit on the oven floor, heat on high for 30 seconds or until just warm, cut in half and squeeze juice. See **grapefruit**; **lemon**; **lime**; **orange**; **satsuma**.

clam A shellfish normally sold live in its shell. Clams can be bought in shell or ready shelled, those in shell need to be washed under cold water before cooking.

TO COOK: place 675 g of clams in a large bowl. Cover the bowl and cook on high for 3–5 minutes, stirring frequently during cooking. **Stand** for 3 minutes. Remove the top shell and serve with garlic butter.

clarified butter   A form of butter that has had its water and milk solids removed. Clarified butter can be used for frying at higher temperatures than normal without the risk of splattering or burning. The microwave oven can be used to clarify butter.

TO CLARIFY: cut the butter into small pieces, cover loosely with kitchen paper and heat on high until melted. Skim off the solids that rise to the surface and pour off the clear liquid, carefully leaving the milky solids behind. Alternatively, strain the liquid butter through a muslin if preferred.

clarify   To make clear by heating. See **clarified butter**.

cleaning a microwave oven   The interior walls of a microwave oven do not heat up so any splashing or spilled foods do not bake on and can be quickly and easily wiped off. It is important to keep the oven cavity clean because any foods that get spilled inside will absorb microwave energy and start to slow down the normal cooking process. Use a cloth soaked in warm soapy water to wipe the inside, remove any detachable parts, such as the turntable, and wash separately, and pay particular attention to the door seal area. Remove stubborn stains by bringing a bowl of water to the boil, the steam produced will help loosen the food. To remove lingering smells from the oven, place a bowl containing 250 ml of water, a few sprigs of thyme or 2 lemon slices and heat on high for 3 minutes or until boiling.

Wipe the outside of the oven with a damp cloth, and when cleaning the touch-control panel, be sure to open the door first to prevent the oven from starting accidentally. For combination ovens, follow the manufacturers' recommended cleaning methods given in the handbook.

clingfilm A type of plastic wrapping material used to cover food for storage purposes. Manufacturers are now producing a microwave-safe polythene film, which does not contain additives that can move from the plastic into the food when heated. Always look for the label 'suitable for the microwave'. If there is no such label do not use the clingfilm in a microwave.

Clingfilm is very useful for covering food and containers in the microwave. However, make sure that the film and the food do not come into direct contact. A tight covering of clingfilm will trap the steam produced, which means that the food can be cooked more quickly. It also stops the evaporation of cooking liquids or the moisture in the food. Always pierce the clingfilm after cooking to allow the hot steam to escape before uncovering the food.

If the food needs to be stirred during the cooking, either remove the film, stir and then replace with fresh film, or cut a slit and stir through that, re-covering the whole with a piece of clingfilm. See also **covering food**.

clove Whole cloves are the dried unopened buds of a small, aromatic evergreen tree. Cloves have an aroma that is spicy, peppery, sweet, fruity, woody and musty. Whole cloves give a delicious flavour to apple pie, whole baked onions and bread sauce. Ground cloves are useful in fruit cakes, various sauces and vegetable dishes. See also **spices**.

coalfish See **saithe**.

cocoa A fine, dark brown powder obtained by roasting and grinding husked cocaa beans (the seeds of the cacoa tree). Cocoa powder is used to flavour biscuits, cakes and desserts. It is commonly used to make a hot drink.

TO MAKE: heat on high 240 ml of milk, or milk and water, in the microwave, allowing $1\frac{1}{2}$ minutes. Then mix with the cocoa powder, stir until blended and add sugar to taste.

coconut The white meat inside the fruit of the coconut palm, which can be eaten fresh or dried (desiccated coconut). It is used for flavouring cakes, desserts and ice cream. Creamed coconut is bought as a solid mass and can be softened in boiling water for use in curries and sauces, particularly Malaysian dishes.

TO TOAST: spread 100 g of desiccated coconut on a plate. Cook on high for 4–6 minutes and stir every minute.

TO COOK: coconut milk can be prepared in the microwave. Put 100 g of unsweetened, shredded or desiccated coconut into a bowl, and then pour over 250 ml of hot water or milk. Cover the bowl and cook on high for 5–6 minutes. Allow the mixture to cool, then strain as much liquid as possible from the coconut. This mixture should yield about 175 ml.

cod A large North Atlantic white fish, usually sold as fillets or steaks. Cod is an excellent fish for cooking in the microwave because it is moist with firm flesh and good flavour. A little lemon juice or butter may be added before cooking. Cod fillet is best cooked skinned.

TO COOK: arrange fillets in a shallow dish with the thickest part towards the outside, they can overlap if necessary. Cover the dish and cook 225 g of fillet for 2 minutes on high or 450 g for 2–3 minutes. **Stand** for 2 minutes.

To cook cod steaks, arrange these with the thinner parts towards the centre. Cover and cook as for the fillets, although the steaks need a little extra time, 4 minutes per 450 g on high.

coffee   A dark liquid made from coffee beans. Coffee can be bought as whole roasted beans, ready ground beans or instant coffee.

TO FRESHEN: coffee beans in the microwave, put 25 g of beans into a bowl, heat for 45 seconds on high then grind and use to make coffee.

TO REHEAT: pour the coffee into individual heat-resistant, non-metallic cups or a jug. Heat on high, 1 cup for $1\frac{1}{2}$–2 minutes, 2 cups for $2\frac{1}{2}$–$3\frac{1}{2}$ minutes. Do not allow the coffee to boil and add the milk, if desired, after heating.

combination oven   An oven in which microwave and conventional energies are used simultaneously, or in sequence, in the same oven cavity. Combination ovens are particularly good for roasting and baking, because the microwave energy provides speed combined with conventional browning. A whole meal can be produced in a very short space of time with the appearance of traditionally cooked food. It is possible to use metal containers in combination ovens, so that frozen convenience foods can be defrosted and reheated in their original foil containers. Normal cake tins and baking trays can also be used as long as they do not touch each other or the sides of the oven.

comparative power output Microwave ovens can vary from one another in power output. Machines offering variable power control also use different systems to describe their various power levels. When using microwave recipes, check the microwave power level recommended and compare them with those of your own oven and adjust if necessary. For example, if a recipe gives a time based on 650 W output and your oven is 500 W, then cooking time will need to be increased by 25 seconds for each minute given, and for a 600 W oven by 10 seconds per minute. For a 700 W oven, the time must be decreased by 15 seconds per minute.

If in doubt about the timings it is always better to undercook. Then allow the food to stand and check whether it is cooked. Once something has been overcooked it cannot be rectified. See also **variable power control**; **wattage**.

composition of food Fats and sugars absorb microwave energy faster then other liquids, therefore they cook and reach a higher temperature faster than water-based foods. It takes longer to cook foods that are high in moisture, such as meat and vegetables, than it does to cook foods with little water content like cakes.

condensed milk A milk reduced by evaporation to a thick concentration and with sugar added. Condensed milk is thick and sticky and is commonly used in desserts, ice cream, cheesecakes and some sauces.

conduction In microwave terms this is the transmission of microwave energy through the deeper layers of food, which will then heat it through.

confectionery It is very safe and simple to make sweets in the microwave because with no direct heat, there is less danger of burning. Care is needed when boiling sugar and it is best to use large, deep containers to prevent mixtures from boiling over. A sugar thermometer is very useful to test for boiling point and to avoid overcooking, but do not put it in the microwave. Sweets such as mint imperials, coconut ice, peanut brittle, nougat and Turkish delight are a few examples of confectionery that can be made in the microwave.

conserve See jam.

convenience food Any of a variety of foods that may be prepared quickly, with little cooking or reheating. Many ready made foods can be reheated in the microwave. Canned soups, baked beans, spaghetti, pre-prepared chilled and frozen meals and pizzas are just a few examples of the many types of convenience foods available. Anything in foil or a can must be removed from the packaging. All frozen and chilled meals have cooking instructions for the microwave, which must be followed. It is very important to cook the foods to the full recommended time to ensure that the dish is fully reheated. Foods frozen in sauce and wrapped in boil-in-the-bag packs reheat well. Remember to pierce the bag before cooking and stir during the cooking to ensure an even distribution of heat through the sauce.

converting recipes for the microwave Many conventional recipes can be converted for use in the microwave simply by adjusting, and often shortening, the recipe cooking time. First check that all the ingredients can be cooked in the microwave, and look up cooking times for basic ingredients to work out the general overall cooking time of the recipe. In many cases foods cooked in the microwave take about one quarter to one third of conventional cooking time. Remember that foods will continue cooking during **standing time**. Check the food regularly, stir, rearrange and turnover as recommended. Use less liquid when cooking stews, casseroles and soups and especially when cooking vegetables. Reduce flavourings like herbs and spices a little because the flavours of these are enhanced by microwave cooking.

cooking fats/oils All the **fats** and **oils** used in conventional recipes can be used in food cooked in the microwave, but never use fats and oils to deep fry in a microwave. The amounts used in many dishes can be considerably reduced.

cooking techniques To get the best results from microwave cooking various techniques have been developed to enable microwaves to reach every part of the food, to cook evenly, and look attractive. See **arranging food; browning agent; covering food; elevating foods; piercing; rearranging food; rotating dish; shielding; standing time; stirring; turning food; whisking**.

cooking time There are various factors that affect cooking time: the microwave oven power output; the nature and quantity of the food; the container used and the recipe method. See **composition of food; density of food; quantity of food; shape and size of food; temperature of food**.

cookware Dishes that are suitable for microwave cooking should not act as a barrier to microwave energy nor should they absorb the energy. A vast range of specially designed

microwave cookware is available, but for
general use many everyday kitchen items can
be used in the microwave including casseroles,
bowls and dishes made from heatproof glass,
glass-ceramic, china, and pottery free from
metal. Plastic containers (suitable for the
microwave; ordinary plastic containers will
melt), paper goods and other natural materials,
such as wicker (basket), can be used for short-
term heating.

To test cookware for microwave safety, pour
cold water into a 250 ml glass bowl or jug and
place it in the microwave next to the dish or
utensil to be tested. Heat on high for 1–2
minutes. The water should be warm, the dish or
utensil cool. If the dish is warm do not use it
because it contains moisture, which is attrac-
ting some of the microwave energy and preventing it from reaching the food. See **bacon
rack**; **browning dish**; **china**; **deep bun dish**; **divided dish**; **glass**; **paper**; **plastic**; **pottery**; **ramekin**;
ring mould; **roasting dish**; **stacking ring**.

cookware shapes and sizes Round and ring
shapes give the most even cooking results,
whereas square and oval shapes have a tendency to overcook in the corners. Since the
penetration of microwave energy is to a depth
of about 5 cm, shallow dishes give better
cooking results than deeper dishes. A straight-
sided container is better than a curved one,

because microwaves can penetrate more evenly.

Choose deep bowls when cooking foods that require a large quantity of boiling water, for example, pasta, rice and pulses, and allow space for food to swell. Some foods rise during cooking, such as cakes or milk-based sauces, so use a jug or bowl large enough to allow for any expansion. In general do not use a dish that is too large because the food spreads out thinly and overcooks at the edges. Most recipes with servings for four can be cooked in medium-sized containers.

coriander   The dried ripe seeds of a Eurasian plant. Coriander is used whole or ground, and has a slightly burnt orange flavour. The leaves of the coriander have a similar appearance to flat-leaved parsley and have a strong aroma. They are used in many Middle Eastern and Asian dishes, and as a garnish to many other spicy dishes. See **herbs**; **spices**.

cornflour   A fine, starchy flour made from maize and used for thickening foods, especially sauces. Cornflour is very useful for preparing food in the microwave, a casserole for example can always be thickened at the end of cooking time with the addition of a little blended cornflour.

cornmeal See **polenta**.

corn oil The yellow-coloured vegetable oil extracted from maize and used for cooking and salad dressings.

corn on the cob See **sweetcorn**.

courgette A small variety of marrow with thin, shiny, dark green skin and white flesh. Select straight, firm courgettes with bright, unwrinkled skin; trim both ends and wash. Cook small courgettes whole, but slice, halve or quarter the larger ones.

TO COOK: place in a dish with a dot of butter or margarine (they do not need any extra water), add herbs and seasoning for extra flavour. Cover and cook 225 g for 4–5 minutes on high and 450 g for 5–7 minutes, and stir or shake twice during cooking. Allow to **stand** for 3 minutes.

couscous Tiny cream-coloured pellets, made from semolina moistened and coated with flour. Serve couscous with fruity spiced meat and stews, traditionally eaten with mutton or chicken and sometimes fish. They may be served with any meat or vegetable dish, normally with rice or pasta.

TO COOK: place 100 g in a bowl with 300 ml of boiling water and stir well. Cover the bowl and cook on high for 2–3 minutes, then allow to **stand** for 5 minutes. Drain, fork through and season well.

covering food By covering food in the microwave moisture is retained and steam is produced, which helps to shorten the cooking time. A loose cover also prevents any splattering on to the oven walls, especially from fatty foods. As a general guide, food normally covered for conventional cooking is likely to be covered in the microwave. However, dishes that are meant to have a dry finish (e.g. cakes) are best left uncovered, which allows the steam to escape.

When cooking foods that need frequent stirring and rearranging it is easier to use a container with a lid, a plate makes a good substitute as long as it covers the bowl. Alternatively, microwave-safe **clingfilm** can be used, but turn back a corner or pierce a few holes to allow the steam to escape. Always take care when removing lids and clingfilm to lift the cover towards you to avoid scalding steam. Instead of cooking vegetables in a covered dish they can be cooked in a **roasting bag**. See also **greaseproof paper**; **kitchen paper**.

crab A marine crustacean **shellfish**, usually pink or brown with a broad, flat shell, pincers and smooth, delicate sweet-flavoured flesh. The claw meat is usually the choicest. Crab must be cooked conventionally, but the extracted meat can be used in a variety of dishes that can be cooked in the microwave, such as fishcakes and devilled crab.

cracked wheat See **bulgar**.

cranberry The sour, red berry of a variety of trailing shrub. Choose plump, firm, shiny red to reddish-brown berries, which bounce when ripe.

TO COOK: wash 450 g of cranberries, place them in a large bowl and pierce with a fork to prevent them from bursting. Add 30 ml of water, cover the bowl and cook on high for 5 minutes. Then add 225 g of sugar and cook on high for 2 minutes, stirring until the sugar has dissolved. Serve warm or cold.

crayfish (also called **crawfish**) A freshwater crustacean that looks like a small lobster. Crayfish can be bought both raw and cooked, and with or without its head.

TO COOK: place 225 g of raw or cooked crayfish in a dish, cover and cook on high for 1 minute. Allow to **stand** for 3 minutes.

cream The yellow fat that rises to the top of the milk when left to stand. Cream is used in cooking and for adding to desserts.

cream cheese A smooth, soft white cheese made from cream or whole milk and used in cooking especially cheesecake.

TO SOFTEN: place 225 g of cream cheese on a microwave-safe plate and heat on low for $1\frac{1}{2}$–2 minutes, until spreadable.

crevettes See **Mediterranean prawn**.

croissant An enriched bread dough shaped into a crescent. Croissant are commonly eaten warm with butter and preserves for breakfast or brunch. They may also be split and filled with savoury or sweet mixtures for a light snack or dessert.

TO WARM: wrap a croissant in kitchen paper and heat on high for a few seconds.

crouton Crisp cubes of bread added to soups and salads as a garnish. To make croutons, cut two thick slices of bread, trim the crusts and spread both sides with softened butter. Cut into small cubes and spread over the base of a large plate or dish. Cook uncovered on high for 2–3 minutes stirring frequently until firm. Spread on kitchen paper to cool and crisp. It is a good idea to keep an eye on the croutons when cooking because they are easily burnt.

cube Vegetables and meat are often cut into even cubes before cooking. These cubes are usually 1 cm square, unless otherwise stated in the recipe.

cumin The aromatic seeds of a Mediterranean shrub, dried and used whole or ground as a **spice**. The flavour is strong and distinctive, giving a spiciness to foods particularly curry.

curd cheese A smooth, mild-tasting white cheese made from skimmed or semi-skimmed milk, most often used in cheesecakes.

currant A dried blackcurrant used in biscuits and cakes. See **dried fruit**.

curry powder A popular flavouring, consisting of a blend of spices including **coriander**, **chilli**, **cumin**, **ginger**, **turmeric**, which can be bought in varying strengths from mild to hot. It is useful for perking up some bland dishes, but when making curry dishes it is best to use a mixture of fresh spices to give a better flavour.

custard A hot or cold sauce, traditionally made with eggs, milk and sugar, flavoured with vanilla.

TO COOK: to make ordinary custard, mix together 15 ml of caster sugar, 30 ml of custard powder and a dash from 570 ml (1 pint) of milk. Heat the remaining milk on high for 4–5 minutes, then pour it over the custard powder and stir well. Return the mixture to the microwave and cook on high for $1-1\frac{1}{2}$ minutes, stirring frequently.

custard apple (also called **cherimoya**) The heart-shaped **fruit** of a West Indian tree with a thin skin and creamy, pulpy flesh. The sieved flesh (to remove any seeds) may be added to drinks, desserts, cakes, soufflés, crumbles, curries and ice cream, and it also makes an excellent sauce.

dab A small flatfish similar to plaice, but smaller and sold whole or in fillets.

TO COOK: poach in a little wine with herbs, cover and cook 225 g on high for 3–4 minutes and 450 g for 4–5 minutes. **Stand** for 3 minutes. See also **fish**.

damson A small blue-black, plumlike fruit, which generally has a sour taste and thus is most often used either stewed with sugar for puddings or in jams and jellies.

TO COOK: wash the fruit, split and remove stones. Place with the cut side up in a shallow dish. Sprinkle with sugar to taste, cover the dish and cook 225 g for 3 minutes or 450 g for 4–5 minutes, stirring once during cooking. Use in a pie or crumble or serve hot or cold with cream or custard.

dasheen See **taro**.

date The long, oval fruit of the date palm, with thin, shiny, brown skin, crisp, very sweet flesh and a long woody stone. Dates are eaten fresh or dried, or used in cakes and desserts. Dried dates can be cooked and added to other cooked fruit, such as rhubarb and apple.

TO COOK: put 225 g of dried dates into a dish and pour over 150 ml of boiling water. Cover the dish and cook for 3–4 minutes, stirring once. Allow to **stand** for 10–15 minutes.

deep bun dish (also called **muffin tray**) A round tray with a circle of deep holes, usually made from durable plastic. It is used for preparing small cakes and poached eggs. A deep bun dish should be used when baking in the microwave, because the tray supports the sides of the cakes. See also **cookware**.

defrost button A facility on most microwave ovens, which is essential if frozen foods are used regularly. The defrost button causes less energy to be emitted by pulsing it on and off in a regular pattern, or by reducing the overall wattage. On models that do not offer **variable power control** the defrost setting can also be used to cook or reheat delicate foods at a low and gentle speed. See also **defrosting**; **defrost level**.

defrosting One of the main advantages of the microwave is that it can thaw frozen food in minutes. Most manufacturers have incorporated a **defrost button**, which allows food to defrost slowly and evenly without danger of it drying out or cooking at the edges. If the cooker does not have this facility then it is possible to simulate its action by turning it on and off at regular intervals, with rest periods in between until the food is evenly defrosted.

Always defrost food slowly so that it does not begin to cook on the outside before it is completely thawed. Transfer food from foil trays or containers into a suitable microwave dish before defrosting, and remove any metal ties. Use a container the same size as the food; if the food has too much room, it spreads out as it thaws and the edges start to cook.

Pierce any clingfilm, boil-in-the-bag pouches, skins or membranes before defrosting. Break up and stir food blocks as they start to defrost so that frozen parts are brought to the edges. Separate foods such as sausages, beefburgers and fish fingers as they defrost. Melted ice should be drained off as it collects because it continues to attract microwave energy and will slow down thawing. Open all cartons and remove any lids prior to defrosting. Vegetables can be cooked from frozen without being defrosted.

When defrosting food that does not need cooking, e.g. bread, use the defrost setting only, and if the food starts to feel warm leave it to stand for a few minutes then continue. Place bread, cakes or pastry on a double layer of kitchen paper to absorb the excess moisture or use a roasting dish or a trivet. Shield any delicate, thinner parts with small pieces of foil to prevent them cooking while the denser parts are still thawing.

When thawing poultry it is best to remove the bird from its wrapping. Protect the thinner parts, such as wingtips and drumsticks, with a little **foil**. To minimize the risk of **food poisoning** it is essential that poultry is thoroughly thawed before cooking. Test to see whether there are any ice crystals still in the carcass cavity and that the legs and thighs are soft and flexible.

Large items like joints of meat are best defrosted for several minutes at a time then left to stand. This standing time is very important because it allows the temperature to equalize throughout the food. Do not microwave a joint until the centre is completely defrosted otherwise the outer edges start to cook before the rest of the meat.

If defrosting and cooking in one operation then remember to stir the defrosted food or rearrange the food during defrosting and cooking time. See APPENDIX II, THAWING TABLES.

defrost level   Any of the following can represent defrost on microwave ovens: 30–40% of power input, (or that the energy is on for this percentage of time); number 3 or 4; 200–250 watt output; or simmer or stew. See also **variable power level**.

density of food   The denser the food the longer it takes to cook. For example, a joint of meat takes longer to defrost, reheat or cook than light, porous foods such as bread and cakes. When cooking a mixture of dense and light-textured food, arrange the denser food around the edge of the dish where they receive more microwave energy, and place the light-structured food in the centre so that it does not cook too quickly.

dill The leaves and seedlike fruits of a Eurasian shrub, used as a **herb**. Dill is particularly good when added to fish dishes.

dish lining Certain foods, such as pâtés, terrines and meat loaves, must be separated from the dish they are cooked in to prevent sticking. Use microwave-safe **clingfilm** or non-stick paper, which can be cut to fit inside soufflé dishes, cake moulds and any other baking dishes. The paper is not affected by microwaves and can be easily peeled off after the **standing time**.

divided dish A useful microwave dish for heating or cooking several foods at the same time. See also **cookware**.

done A term used to describe food when it has finished cooking. When testing food to see if it has cooked enough the **standing time** must be taken into account, if this is indicated in the recipe. If the food is not properly cooked after completion of the recommended standing time return it to the microwave for another minute or two.

The completed cooking time of joints of meat can be accurately assessed by using a microwave-safe **thermometer** or probe. Alternatively, to test whether poultry is thoroughly cooked pierce the thickest part of the leg and if the juices run clear, without a trace of pink, the bird is done. Small pieces or cubes of meat are ready when a fork easily penetrates the surface through to the bottom. Fish is cooked when the flesh is opaque and flakes easily when tested with a fork. Vegetables should be just tender when pierced with a fork.

Cakes look wet on the surface at the end of cooking time, but after standing time the moist spots dry and the cake begins to pull away from the sides of the mould. To test when a cake is completely ready insert a cocktail stick or skewer into the centre of the cake and it should come out cleanly, or scratch the top with a knife and the exposed surface should be firm. To test a plate of reheated food, feel the bottom of the plate with your hand, if it is hot then the food is heated through, if it is cool, so is the food.

door release　A button or a release catch in the handle of the oven door. When the door is opened the **magnetron** immediately stops producing microwaves, and no microwaves remain inside the oven. This feature is part of the safety system for all microwave ovens. There are up to seven cut-out devices incorporated in micro-waves to ensure that the energy is cut off automatically whenever the door is opened.

door safety catch A safety feature that ensures that the microwave operates only when the door is properly shut.

door seal Microwave oven doors are constructed to precise specifications to ensure that once they are shut, the cooking cavity is completely sealed so that there is no energy leakage. This feature is vital to safety when using microwave ovens.

double oven unit A conventional oven and a microwave oven situated in a unit together. The cooking operations are separate, but the arrangement provides a convenient way to combine two cooking methods, for example, food may be microwaved for speed and then browned in the conventional oven or grill.

Dover sole A particularly solid flatfish with brown-grey skin, white flesh and a good flavour, which is normally sold either whole or in fillets. See **sole**.

dried fruit A variety of fruits are available in a dried form including apples (in slices), bananas, apricots, figs, peaches, pears and prunes. Dried fruits are well suited for microwave cooking because they quickly plump and soften, eliminating the need to pre-soak the fruit. The longer the fruit is left to **stand** after cooking, the richer the flavours.

TO COOK: put the fruit into a bowl and pour over approximately 600 ml of boiling water. Cover the bowl and cook 100 g on high for 5 minutes and 225 g on high for 10–12 minutes, stirring once or twice. Allow to stand 10–30 minutes.

Always prepare dried fruit in a generous amount of water, particularly apple and pear slices, which may need extra water. It is best to avoid cooking more than 100 g at one time because the fruit swell quite considerably during cooking. See also **currants**; **sultanas**; **raisins**.

drinking chocolate A powder of cocoa and sugar to which hot or cold milk is added to make a drink.

TO MAKE: pour 240 ml (8 fluid ounces) of milk into a jug or mug, place in the oven and heat on high for 2 minutes. Add 3 teaspoons of drinking chocolate and stir until blended.

drying herbs Fresh **herbs** can be dried successfully in the microwave for use all year round. It is best to dry about 15 g at a time. Remove the stalks, rinse the leaves and carefully pat dry with absorbent paper. Place the herbs between two sheets of absorbent paper on the turntable or floor of the oven. Add a small bowl of water as a safety measure.

TO DRY: generally heat herbs on high for 3–6 minutes (depending on the type of herb – see individual entries) until they lose their bright colour and become brittle to touch. Rearrange during cooking. Leave them to cool, then crumble and store in an airtight jar.

duck Any of a variety of aquatic birds and their meat, shot as game or raised domestically. The microwave is a good way of cooking duck. Before microwaving, pierce the skin in many places to allow the fat to drain and to prevent the skin from splitting during cooking.

TO COOK: rub salt into the skin of a 1.75 kg (4 lb) prepared duck. Place the bird breast-side down in a **roasting dish**, cover with **greaseproof paper** or a split **roasting bag** and cook on high for 10 minutes. Then drain off any fat and turn the duck over, cover and cook for a further 18 minutes. To crisp and brown the skin, either cover and **stand** for 15 minutes or place in a hot conventional oven for 15 minutes.

To cook duck portions prepare in the same way and use a roasting dish. Cook 4 portions (approximately 300 g each) on high for 20 minutes, turning halfway through the cooking time. Leg portions take longer to cook than breast portions. Brown and crisp the portions under a conventional grill.

egg The mature ovum of a chicken (or other poultry) protected by a calcified shell. All the basic ways of cooking eggs, such as scrambling, poaching, frying, baking, making omelettes and soufflés, work very well in the microwave with the exception of boiled eggs. Never cook an egg in its shell in the microwave. The build up of pressure inside the shell causes expansion and eventually the egg will explode.

TO COOK: eggs cook very fast in a microwave, so careful attention must be paid to timings because they are a delicate food and toughen when over-cooked. The yolks, which have a higher fat content, cook faster than the whites. Bake, fry, or poach eggs on medium, to allow the whites time to set without over-cooking the yolks. Before cooking, pierce the yolk with a cocktail stick to puncture the membrane, otherwise it could burst. Expect eggs to look soft when removed from the microwave, but they will continue to cook during **standing time**.

When yolks and whites are mixed together for scrambled eggs or omelettes they can be cooked on high, but they will still need standing time. If the finished result is not to your liking, return to the oven for 15 seconds at a time.

eggplant See **aubergine**.

elevating food Certain foods, such as crumbles, cakes, meatloaf and quiches, should be raised off the oven floor to allow the microwave energy to cook them thoroughly. Microwave-safe racks or trivets can be used underneath dishes, and roasting racks in deep dishes keep joints of meat from stewing in their own juices. Alternatively, use an inverted saucer or ramekin dish to elevate the dish.

equipment for cooking   See **cookware; microwave tools; thermometer**.

evaporated milk   A thick, unsweetened tinned milk, which has been reduced by evaporating some of the water content. It can be reconstituted by adding water and may be used in place of full-cream milk. It is also used in desserts and savoury dishes.

fats Large organic compounds that are insoluble in water and are found in the body as body fat, and as a nutrient in food with a very high energy value. Since fat attracts microwaves, meat high in fat cooks more quickly than lean meat. See also **composition of food**.

faults in a microwave oven If a microwave oven becomes damaged in any way, do not use it until it has been repaired and checked by a qualified technician. Never attempt to repair any damage yourself. Always contact the manufacturer or dealer if any fault occurs.

features of the microwave oven All ovens consist of a basic unit of a cabinet, with an interior light and a door and frame fitted with special seals. The oven cavity is made from metal providing a surface for the microwaves to bounce off. When the machine is turned on, the microwaves are produced by the **magnetron**. They travel along the **wave guide** and enter the oven. The **wave stirrer** turns slowly to distribute the microwaves in an even pattern and the **air vent** allows any steam to escape during cooking. In addition to the basic unit features there are numerous options available on the microwave. See also **audible reminder**; **autosensor**; **browning grill**; **defrost button**; **door release**; **door seal**; **memory control**; **removable**

floor; **rotating antennae**; **splash guard**; **stirrer fan**; **temperature probe**; **timing control**; **turntable**; **variable power control**; **wattage**.

fennel The seeds and feathery leaves of a strong-smelling, yellow flowered plant, used as a **herb**. The seeds are used particularly in curry, bread, pasta and pickles and go well with fish and poultry.

TO COOK: trim and wash the fennel, slice in half lengthways and place in a dish with 2 tbsp of water. Cover the dish and cook 225 g on high for 4–5 minutes or 450 g for 6–8 minutes. Leave to **stand** for 3 minutes. Cook a little longer if a softer texture is preferred.

fig The pear-shaped **fruit** pod of a tropical and sub-tropical tree, with smooth, fleshy, green or purple skin. Select soft, sweet-smelling figs with undamaged skin. They are best eaten fresh, but they can be used in ice cream and desserts.

filo pastry A wafer-thin type of **pastry**, which is normally purchased already frozen. Filo pastry can be cooked in the microwave, but, as with other pastries, it does not brown and is not always crisp. It is better to cook it conventionally.

fish Any species of marine or freshwater, cold-blooded aquatic vertebrae. The microwave is ideal for cooking fish, the speed of cooking ensures firm, moist flesh without the loss of its delicate flavours. Although fish cooks in its own moisture lemon juice, butter or wine may be added to enhance the flavour. Careful handling is needed to give best results. Whole flatfish, such as **brill**, **dab**, **plaice** and **sole**, are so thin that they do not need to be turned over during the fast cooking time. Fish can be cooked in all the usual microwave containers and also in **roasting bags**, which can be thrown away afterwards.

When cooking whole round fish, such as **trout** or **mullet**, score the sides of the fish on both sides to prevent the skins bursting. Very large fish, such as **salmon**, can be curved round to fit into a round dish, and once cooked the fish remains curved. Cover delicate parts of a whole fish, such as the tail or eyes, with smooth strips of **foil**.

Timing is critical when cooking fish, because over-cooking destroys the delicate flavour and makes the flesh tough. Always cook for the minimum time given in a recipe, then check. If the thinner parts are opaque and the flesh flakes easily allow the fish to **stand** for 3 minutes, by which time the thicker parts will be cooked.

TO COOK: whole fish (e.g. trout, mullet), slash the skins to prevent bursting and shield the tail with foil. Cook for 3 minutes per 450 g on high, and turn over during cooking.

To cook fish fillets, arrange them on a dish, with the thinner parts towards the centre, tucked under or slightly overlapping to give as even a thickness as possible. Cover and cook on high for about 4–5 minutes for 450 g, rearrange the fillets halfway through cooking.

To 'steam' fish portions or steaks quickly, place them in the centre of lightly moistened kitchen paper. Bring all corners to the centre and twist to close, then place in a microwave dish. Cook 1, 225 g fish steak on high for 2–3 minutes, rearranging once, or allow 4–5 minutes per 450 g.

Fish fingers and pieces of fish coated with egg and breadcrumbs can be cooked in a little hot oil, but they need a **browning dish** to crisp them. To cook from frozen allow 3–4 minutes per 100 g and 5–6 minutes per 225 g, turn over and around halfway through. Fish in batter that needs deep frying must not be cooked in the microwave. See **bass**; **bream**; **cod**; **flounder**; **haddock**; **hake**; **halibut**; **herring**; **monkfish**; **octopus**; **pilchard**; **sardine**; **shellfish**; **squid**.

fish stock   A broth or liquid made with fish and vegetables.

TO COOK: put 700 g of white fish bones and pieces into a large bowl with a chopped up half leek, carrot and celery, add 750 ml of water, 250 ml of dry white wine, a few peppercorns and a sprig of parsley. Cover and cook on high for 15 minutes. **Stand** for 5 minutes then strain into a clean bowl.

flageolet An immature green haricot bean, with a delicate flavour, colour and texture.

TO COOK: after soaking, rinse the beans and place them in a large dish and cover with fresh boiling water. Cover the dish and cook 225 g of beans on high for 20–30 minutes, ensuring that the beans are boiling hard for the first 10 minutes, and stir 2 or 3 times during cooking. Leave to **stand** for 5–10 minutes. Cook for a further 5–10 minutes if hard. See also **pulses**.

flounder (also called **fluke**) A European flatfish with a greyish-brown body, soft white flesh and a mild taste. Flounder is often used as a generic term applying to hundreds of different kinds of flatfishes around the world. It can be cooked whole or as fillets.

TO COOK: place whole fish in a dish, add a squeeze of lemon juice and a dot of butter. Cover and cook 450 g for 4–5 minutes. **Stand** for 3 minutes, then serve with a well-flavoured sauce.

flour Finely or coarsely ground cereals, especially wheat, which is used to make a variety of foods, including bread, biscuits, and pasta.

fluke   See **flounder**.

foil   A very thin sheet of aluminium for use in cooking and food storage. Foil may be used to protect thinner parts of a food, see **shielding**. However, the amount of food uncovered must be greater than the amount covered. There must be enough food exposed to absorb all the microwave energy. Foil can be added to the food halfway through cooking or to areas once they are cooked and during the standing time.

It is important that foil is never allowed to touch the sides of the oven cavity, because this would cause **arcing**. If any piece of foil comes loose during cooking switch the oven off immediately and remove it.

food poisoning   An acute illness caused by foods or substances in them, and characterized by gastrointestinal inflammation, vomiting and diarrhoea. Food poisoning may be caused by bacteria (e.g. **listeria** and **salmonella**), moulds, chemicals or toxic substances that occur naturally in foods. Always choose the freshest food available and ensure that chilled foods are kept cool from the shop to home. Cook as soon as possible after purchase. Store raw foods and dairy products at the correct temperature in the refrigerator. Always store raw foods wrapped, and well away from cooked foods to prevent any cross-contamination. Because of the high temperatures reached in a microwave, thorough cooking destroys all bacteria including salmonella and listeria. Check that food is always completely cooked and do not leave uneaten cooked food standing at room temperature, once it has been cooked, cover and refrigerate.

frankfurter A light brown, smoked sausage made of finely minced pork or beef and mildly seasoned. Commonly eaten in a bread roll as a 'hot dog'. Pre-cooked frankfurters can be eaten cold, but are more often served hot.

TO COOK: pierce the skins to prevent the frankfurters bursting, and place in a suitable dish. Cook 1 frankfurter on high for 30 seconds, 2 for 40 seconds and 4 for 1 minute.

freezer bag A polythene bag designed for use in the freezer. A freezer bag may be used for reheating small quantities of leftovers, or to steam and tenderize food (pierce the bag if instructed in the recipe). However, it can only be used for short periods of defrosting and reheating without melting.

Never use plastic bags that are not specifically designed for microwave use. Some will melt and others, at high temperatures, may release their plasticisers into the food. If in doubt about the suitability of a bag do not use it.

French bean The slender, green pods of a small twining plant, an immature **pulse**. Many varieties have been produced including the shorter and plumper Bobby bean.

TO COOK: top and tail, and cook whole or cut into short lengths. Put the beans into a dish with 3 tbsp of water, cover and cook 225 g for 5–6 minutes and 450 g for 7–8 minutes on high. **Stand** for 3 minutes.

frogs' legs The legs of a frog bred specifically for eating. Frogs' legs have a texture similar to chicken and are usually available frozen. Once thawed keep them in the refrigerator for up to 3 days.

TO COOK: first melt 25 g of butter in a dish on high for 30 seconds and then add 225 g of frogs' legs. Cover the dish and cook on high for 3–4 minutes, turning the legs once. The juices and butter can be made into a sauce with white wine if desired.

frozen food A method of food preservation. There is only a minimal loss of flavour, texture and nutrients when freezing food. Frozen food can be defrosted in a matter of minutes in the microwave, which is both time saving and convenient. Some foods, such as vegetables, can be defrosted (see **defrosting**) and cooked in one programme. Small quantities of fresh vegetables can also be **blanched** in the microwave for storage in the freezer. See APPENDIX II, THAWING TABLES; APPENDIX III, REHEATING FROM FROZEN CHART. Readers are also recommended to consult the Collins *Gem Food for Freezing*.

fruit The fleshy, ripened ovary of a flowering plant, containing one or more seeds. Compared to conventional cooking, fruit cooked in the microwave keeps its shape better and looks more attractive. If a recipe requires a soft purée, just cook the fruits for a few minutes longer. A wide range of fruits both fresh and dried, some with added sugar, can be quickly prepared to be served hot or cold, and can be used as a base for steamed puddings and crumbles, ice creams, sauces and purées.

Fruit with a firm skin, such as **apples**, need to be scored or pricked, so that they do not burst during cooking. Whole firm fruits, such as **apricots**, **cherries**, **peaches**, **nectarines** and **pears**, are delicious when poached in a sugar syrup. Peaches, apricots and nectarines do not need skinning before microwaving, because the skin peels away easily after cooking. See **acorn squash**; **babaco**; **banana**; **blackberry**; **blackcurrant**; **blueberry**; **butternut squash**; **cherry**; **citrus fruit**; **gooseberry**; **grapefruit**; **greengage**; **kiwi fruit**; **loganberry**; **mango**; **plum**; **raspberry**; **redcurrant**; **rhubarb**; **strawberry**.

fruit pie   Cooked fruit pie can be reheated in
the microwave. Place the pie in a suitable container with thinner parts (if any) to the centre.
   TO COOK: place in the oven uncovered, heat on
high for 30 seconds for 1 serving, 45 seconds for
2 servings, and $1\frac{1}{2}$ minutes for 4 servings. Take
care when eating because the fruit is much
hotter than the pastry.

game Any animal, or bird that is shot for sport and eaten. Young game birds can be cooked in the microwave, but older tougher ones are best casseroled conventionally. Do not overcook or the flesh will dry out and toughen. The flesh needs a little fat to prevent it drying out, so use butter or slices of bacon. Cooking in a roasting bag will help keep the flesh moist. See **grouse**; **hare**; **pheasant**; **pigeon**; **quail**; **rabbit**.

gammon The cured leg of a pig, usually the foreleg, which may be smoked or unsmoked (green). A gammon joint cooked in the microwave keeps its shape and flavour, and is especially successful if it is to be served cold. Unless the joint is one of the pre-shaped round kinds, it should be soaked overnight in two or three changes of cold water to remove any excess salt. For larger pieces gentler cooking produces the best results, allowing the centre to cook without hardening the outer edges.

TO COOK: put into a pierced **roasting bag**, place in a **roasting dish** and cook on high, allowing 10–12 minutes per 450 g, turning over and round during cooking. **Stand** for 15 minutes in tented **foil**. If the joint is unevenly shaped, shield the thinner end with foil half-way through cooking. To glaze fat, remove the rind after cooking, score with a sharp knife, brush with honey or warm marmalade and brown under a hot grill. If using a thermometer the final temperature should be 60°C (160°F).

To cook gammon rashers or steaks, remove the rind and snip the fat at intervals, so that the meat does not curl up during cooking. Place on a **bacon rack** and cover with absorbent kitchen paper. Cook 1, 100 g gammon steak for 2–2½ minutes, 2, 100 g steaks for 4–4½ minutes, and 4, 100 g steaks for 6–7 minutes, all on high. Stand for 2 minutes.

garden pea See **pea**.

garlic The bulb of a small Asian plant, divided into many separate 'cloves'. Garlic is used fresh, as a paste, in a tube, dried and powdered or as a salt, to give flavour to food. Include in all types of savoury food especially in dishes of Mediterranean countries, Asian countries, India, Spain and Mexico.

garlic bread Cooked in the microwave garlic bread is moderately successful, but it lacks the familiar crunchy crust of oven-baked or reheated French bread. It is not possible to get a crisp outside with a soft inside in the microwave, it is either all soft or all crisp.

TO COOK: brush thick slices of French bread all over with melted garlic butter and arrange in a **roasting dish**. Cook on high for 2 minutes, then transfer to a wire rack to cool and crisp.

gelatin or **gelatine**   A colourless or yellowish, water-soluble protein, manufactured commercially by boiling animal hides and bones. Powdered gelatin is creamy and granular in colour. In sufficient quantities it forms a solid jelly when it cools and is used to thicken, aerate or set mixtures. A vegetarian alternative to gelatin, agar agar, is available from health food stores.

TO COOK: sprinkle gelatin over measured liquid in a small bowl. Allow to stand for 1 minute until the liquid is absorbed by the gelatin, which becomes spongy. Heat on high for 1 minute, stirring until dissolved. Gelatin's gelling properties are impaired if it is boiled. Allow to cool slightly before mixing into other ingredients. See also **aspic**.

ginger   The underground stem of an Indian plant with a spicy, pungent flavour, which may be bought fresh, dried or ground. Fresh ginger has a strong, citrus-like smell and flavour as well as the characteristic ginger 'hotness', and is used in Chinese, Caribbean and Indian dishes. Avoid adding fresh ginger before prolonged cooking because it will give the food a hot flavour without any fruity freshness. Five minutes or so in a microwave is enough.

Dried ginger root is used in making preserves and chutneys and powdered ginger is a popular flavouring for cakes and biscuits. Ginger may also be crystallized in sugar or preserved in syrup, both excellent for adding to ice cream, cakes, fruit salads and compote of dried fruits.

glass Special microwave-safe glass is available for cooking at high temperatures. Glass-ceramic containers can be used in the microwave, which may also be used as attractive serving dishes because they usually have glass covers that can be used as lids. Any **cookware** made from very thin glass must be used with caution and never use lead crystal in the microwave.

glaze A shiny coating, made from a variety of ingredients, applied to the surface of foods. The appearance of microwaved food can often be improved with the application of a glaze. Glazing with **marmalade** or a specially prepared fruit or honey glaze can improve the flavour and appearance of **gammon** joints and steaks. Brushing whole **chickens** or joints with a glaze, such as honey barbecue, or melted butter or margarine mixed with spices, can be used. Brush the food towards the end of the cooking time, because if the glaze is applied too early it may burn.

globe artichoke The large, thistle-like flower head of an Asian plant. A globe artichoke resembles an unopened round flower bud, with green, purple or bronze-coloured tightly wrapped leaves. Choose compact, heavy, plump globes.

TO COOK: slice the stem off and remove the coarse, lower leaves. The sharp tips of the leaves may be trimmed with scissors if wished. Brush the cut surfaces with lemon juice to prevent darkening. Place in a large **roasting bag** or covered dish with 4 tbsp of water and 1 tbsp of lemon juice. Cook on high allowing 5–6 minutes for 1 head, and 7–8 minutes for 2 heads, depending on size and weight. Turn once during cooking. To test if cooked pull off one of the leaves, it should come away easily. Drain and **stand** for 3–5 minutes.

Before serving, the prickly leaves can be pulled out of the centre and the fuzzy, hairy choke scraped out and discarded. Serve with French dressing or hollandaise sauce.

golden syrup A syrup made from sugar syrup that has been partially broken down into glucose and fructose. Golden syrup is widely used in microwave baking particularly in flapjacks and gingerbread. Syrup bought in microwave-proof plastic or glass jars can be softened in the microwave to make measuring easier. Warm through on the **defrost** setting for 1 minute.

goose The rich, fatty flesh of the goose. The weight of birds usually ranges between 3.25 kg

(7lb) and 6.75 kg (15lb). Although goose can be cooked in a microwave they are often too large (particularly for ovens with turntables) and too fatty to be cooked successfully, and a better result would be achieved in a conventional oven. Choose a young, tender goose without much fat if it has to be cooked in a microwave.

TO COOK: prick the skin so that the fat can drain away. Place the goose breast-side down in a **roasting dish**. Cover with **greaseproof paper** or a split **roasting bag**, and cook on high allowing about 7 minutes per 450 g (1lb). Drain off the juices and turn over halfway through the cooking time. Cover and **stand** for 20 minutes.

gooseberry The pale green or deep red fruit of a Eurasian shrub. Dessert gooseberries need topping and tailing before eating. Cooking varieties can be stewed and made into pies and crumbles or puréed and added to cold custard and cream to make a fool. Prick their skins with a fork or they explode in the microwave.

TO COOK: put 450 g of prepared gooseberries into a shallow dish and add 2 tbsp of water and 100 g of sugar. Cover the dish and cook on high for 4–5 minutes. **Stand** for 2 minutes. For purée, cook a further 2–3 minutes until the fruit softens completely and collapses.

grapefruit A large ruby or yellow **citrus fruit** with yellow or pink flesh. Grapefruit is usually eaten raw, but it can also be halved and served hot. Choose a heavy fruit with bright coloured skin and no brown patches.

TO COOK: cut a grapefruit in half and slice between the membrane of each segment to release them from the pith. Sprinkle with brown sugar, place in a shallow dish and cook on high for 2 minutes, turning the grapefruit round halfway through cooking. Serve hot.

gravy The juices from roasting meat or poultry, which form a sediment and once the fat is poured off are diluted with stock or vegetable cooking water. Gravy may be thickened with flour or cornflour. Commercial gravy powders are a combination of thickening agents, colourings and flavourings, some artificial and some natural. To reheat gravy, cook 300 ml for 4–5 minutes on high.

gravy browning A substance used to enhance the colour of brown gravy made from meat juices. Brushing gravy browning on meat or poultry before cooking in the microwave improves its appearance by giving it a richer colour. See also **browning agent**.

greaseproof paper A type of wrapping material, which can be used to loosely cover food in the microwave to prevent splattering on the oven walls. Whole **fish** and fish steaks can be wrapped into a greaseproof paper parcel before cooking. This is an excellent way to cook fish because the moisture and flavours become trapped inside the parcel.

greengage A small, plumlike fruit with thin, green skin, sweet juicy flesh and a hard stone. Choose firm ripe fruit and remove any stalks. Greengages can be cooked whole or halved and stoned. They are excellent when poached whole in syrup.

TO COOK: put into a dish with 1 tbsp of water, cover and cook 225 g for 3–4 minutes and 450 g for 4–5 minutes on high, stirring once during cooking. **Stand** for 3 minutes.

grilling See **browning grill**.

groundnut See **peanut**.

grouse A game bird available between 12th August and 10th December. Allow one grouse per person.

TO COOK: cover the wings, leg tips and the breastbone with smooth pieces of **foil** to prevent over cooking. Put the bird into a pierced **roasting bag**, and place breast-side down in a **roasting dish**. Cook on medium allowing 7–9 minutes per 450 g and turn over halfway through cooking. If using a thermometer, remove the grouse when it reads 82–85°C.

Allow to **stand** for 15 minutes when the temperature rises to 85–87°C. During standing time always **tent** a grouse with foil to keep it warm. To test if the bird is done, pierce the thickest part of the thigh with a skewer and the juices should run clear without a trace of pink.

guava The small, pale yellow **fruit** of a tropical American tree. Select firm, undamaged fruit with green-yellow skin. Peel, slice or dice the fruit and add to a fruit salad, fruit tart, ice cream, sorbet, jelly or make into jam.

guinea fowl A domestic and game bird with the flavour of gamey chicken.

TO COOK: place a knob of butter in the body cavity. Put the bird breast-side down in a **roasting dish** and cover with a slit or pierced **roasting bag**. Cook on medium for 7–8 minutes per lb and turn over halfway through cooking. Protect any parts that overcook with small pieces of **foil**. Cover and **stand** for 5 minutes.

haddock An Atlantic white fish, similar to cod, but with a finer flavour. Smoked haddock is similarly cooked with the addition of a little butter.

TO COOK: arrange fillets in a shallow dish, with the thickest parts towards the outside, they can overlap if necessary. Cover the dish and cook 225 g of fillets on high for 2 minutes or 450 g for 2–3 minutes. **Stand** for 2 minutes.

To cook haddock steaks, arrange these with the thinner parts towards the centre. Cover and cook as with the fillets, although they need a little extra time, 4 minutes per 450 g on high.

haggis A traditional Scottish dish made from sheep's or calf's offal, oats, and suet tightly packed into a skin made from the animal's stomach and boiled.

TO COOK: remove the skin because it is usually secured with metal tags, which would explode in the microwave. Put a 450 g haggis into a deep bowl and pour in 1–2 pints of cold water. Cover the bowl and cook on high for 10 minutes. Turn the haggis over and continue to cook on medium for a further 15 minutes. **Stand** for 15 minutes.

hake A marine fish with white flesh, similar to cod, sold as cutlets. Add herbs, garlic or lemon to taste.

TO COOK: arrange cutlets in a shallow dish, with the thickest parts towards the outside, they can overlap if necessary. Cover the dish and cook 225 g on high for 2 minutes or 450 g for 2–3 minutes. **Stand** for 2 minutes.

halibut A North Atlantic white fish, the largest flattish, sold in fillets or steaks. Smaller fish are available whole.

TO COOK: place halibut steaks in a dish and add a little wine if preferred. Cover the dish tightly and cook 225 g on high for 2½–3 minutes and 450 g for 4–5 minutes. **Stand** for 2 minutes.

ham See **gammon**.

hamburger See **beefburger**.

hare A game mammal, with darker, richer flesh than rabbit. Hare is seasonal and is usually only available between August and February. Young hares can be roasted, but older animals need to be stewed conventionally ('jugged') in their own juices. Hare joints cook well in the microwave with vegetables and stock.

TO COOK: add the other ingredients according to the recipe used and cook on medium allowing 12–15 minutes per 450 g of meat. Halfway through cooking turn over and rearrange the portions. **Stand** for 5 minutes.

haricot beans The ripe seed of a variety of French bean, which is dried, cooked and eaten as a vegetable or canned in tomato sauce (see **baked bean**).

TO COOK: after soaking, rinse the beans and place them in a large dish and cover with fresh boiling water. Cover the dish and cook 225 g on high for 20–30 minutes, ensuring that the beans are boiling hard for the fist 10 minutes, stirring 2 or 3 times during cooking. Leave to **stand** for 5–10 minutes. Cook for a further 5–10 minutes if still hard. See also **pulses**.

hazelnut (also called **cob nut**) The small, light brown nut of the hazel shrub. Use shelled hazelnuts whole or chopped, for snacks, in cakes, biscuits and stuffings; or grind in a food processor or blender and use in pastry and confectionery, ice cream and desserts.

heart A type of offal, usually from a calf or lamb. Hearts are very tough and are best chopped and used in stews. Lamb and calf heart can be stuffed and braised. Allow 1 heart per serving, remove arteries and tendons before stuffing, and secure with a wooden cocktail stick.

TO COOK: place in a dish, add stock and chopped vegetables. Cover the dish and cook 450 g on medium for 45 minutes. Turn and stir halfway through cooking and **stand** for 10 minutes.

heat equalizing See **standing time**.

herb Any of various aromatic plants used to add flavour to food. Herbs may be used fresh or dried, whole or ground. Fresh herbs have the best flavour and once picked they should be kept in a jar of water or loosely wrapped in a polythene bag in the fridge. Fresh herbs should be lightly washed and patted dry before use. Use them whole, or chopped, whichever the recipe suggests. Herbs can be chopped on a board with a sharp knife or cut with scissors.

Dried herbs (see **drying herbs**) are more strongly flavoured than fresh ones so only a smaller quantity is required, about a quarter to a third of the amount of fresh herbs. Dried herbs can be added to a dish at the beginning of cooking, but fresh herbs are best added towards the end.

Chopped fresh herbs can add a lift to ordinary sauces for vegetables. Mix them into butter or margarine to make an interesting spread for sandwiches, or use to dress vegetables. See **basil**; **bay leaf**; **chive**; **coriander**; **dill**; **marjoram**; **mint**; **oregano**; **parsley**; **rosemary**; **sage**; **tarragon**; **thyme**.

herb mix See **browning agent**.

herring A marine, soft-finned fatty fish. Fresh herrings should have a shine to their skins and be firm to touch. Cut and gut the fish, remove heads if preferred and score the skin two or three times with a sharp knife to prevent bursting. To get a crisp skin use a preheated **browning dish**.

TO COOK: arrange herrings in a dish, cover with greaseproof paper and cook on high allowing 5–6 minutes for 2, 175 g fish, turning and rearranging halfway. **Stand** for 3 minutes. See also **roe**.

high power level Most recipes, for speed and convenience, require the oven to be used on a high- or full-power level, that is working at maximum cooking speed. High-power level represents 100% power input or it can be the highest number on the dial or control panel. See also **variable power control**.

honey A sweet substance made by bees from flower nectar. Honey's colour and flavour varies depending on the type of flowers the bees have visited, and the way it is processed determines its consistency. Apart from its extensive use in baking and as a spread, honey is often used to sweeten a whole range of dishes.

TO SOFTEN: crystallized honey, remove the lid from jar, heat on high for 1 minute and stir until honey loses its granular texture and is smooth. Heat a little longer if necessary.

hot spot A particular point in some microwaves where there is a concentration of microwaves. Although microwave ovens have **stirrer fans**, **turntables** or **rotating antennae** to help distribute the microwave energy evenly, some ovens may have areas where the food will cook faster. There are techniques, such as turning a dish or rearranging the food during cooking, that help to ensure that the food cooks evenly despite the existence of any hot spots in the oven.

ice cream A sweet frozen food traditionally made with cream, egg yolks and sugar, and often flavoured with fruits. Most home-made ice cream is made with a custard base, which is then flavoured. The custard can be made successfully in the microwave.

TO SOFTEN: ice cream before serving, warm on **defrost** for 30–60 seconds (depending on the amount to be used). This is especially necessary for home-made ice cream, which is often very hard straight from the freezer.

jam (also called **conserve**) A confection of fresh fruit and sugar boiled together until set. It is possible to make small quantities of jam in the microwave. Fruits with a high pectin content set well, such as **blackcurrants**, **redcurrants**, **apples** and **gooseberries**. **Raspberries**, **cherries** and **strawberries** have a medium to low pectin content so some lemon juice or commercial pectin must be added to help achieve a good set.

The fruit must be cooked until soft before the sugar is added. Place the fruit and sugar in a bowl large and deep enough to allow the mixture to bubble up when boiling (remember to use oven gloves when moving the bowl). Once the sugar has been added and thoroughly dissolved the jam is boiled rapidly to setting point, stirring occasionally. To test whether the jam has reached its setting point place a small amount onto a saucer and leave until cold. Then push the surface of the jam and if it wrinkles it is ready. When the jam is ready pour it into hot, sterilized jars.

To sterilize glass jars, half fill them with water and heat in the microwave until they reach boiling point. Then take the jars out and swirl the water around inside, empty and turn upside down on absorbent kitchen paper.

jelly A fruit-flavoured, clear dessert set with **gelatin**. Commercially produced jelly, in the form of cubes, can be dissolved in water in the microwave. Put the jelly into a bowl with 150 ml of water, heat on high for 2 minutes and stir until dissolved. Add the rest of the water and stir together before pouring into a mould to set.

Jerusalem artichoke The tuber of a variety of North American sunflower, with a smooth and pleasant taste and resembling a knobbly potato. The best Jerusalem artichokes should be large, firm, clean and crisp. They may be peeled either before or after cooking. If prepared before, cut off the smaller knobbles with the peel, then place straight into cold water with a little lemon juice to prevent discoloration.

TO COOK: cut the artichokes into thick slices and put them into a dish with 2 tbsp of water. Cover the dish and cook on high allowing 5–6 minutes for 225 g and 8–9 minutes for 450 g. **Stand** for 3 minutes.

julienne Strips of vegetable, usually 5 cm in length and 3 mm thick.

juniper The small, purple berries of a coniferous shrub. Juniper berries are used to give flavour to food and in the making of gin. Before cooking them lightly crush the berries with a rolling pin to split the skin. Their piquant flavour enhances many **game** and **duck** dishes and it also goes well with **goose**, **pork** and **turkey**. Juniper berries are often used in **marinades** and are an essential ingredient in making sauerkraut.

kale A variety of cabbage with slightly bitter, dark green, crinkled leaves. Kale has a strong flavour and is best eaten when young. Remove any tough stalks and shred before cooking.

TO COOK: place the shredded kale in a dish with 2 tbsp of water. Cover the dish and cook 225 g on high for 2–4 minutes and 450 g for 4–6 minutes. Drain well and serve with a little butter or margarine.

kidney A type of **offal** from a lamb, calf, pig or ox. Calf and ox kidneys are only used in slow-cooked stews and pies. Lamb and pig kidneys must have the outer membrane and the inner white core removed, by halving horizontally and snipping it out.

TO COOK: melt 25 g of butter in a microwave dish and then add the kidneys. Cover the dish and cook on high for 3–4 minutes for 225 g and 6–8 minutes for 450 g, stirring halfway through the cooking time. **Stand** for 3 minutes. To tell if the kidneys are correctly cooked, they should be slightly tinged with pink in the centre. They are delicious seasoned with salt and pepper and served on hot toast.

kidney bean See **black kidney bean**; **red kidney bean**.

kipper A salted, smoked herring, which can be successfully cooked in the microwave and with the added advantage that the smell is contained within the oven.

TO COOK: place a kipper in a buttered dish skin-side down, then dot with butter and cover. Cook 450 g on high for 3–4 minutes, turning over halfway through the cooking time.

kitchen paper An absorbent paper that is very useful for soaking up excess moisture or fat when microwaving foods, especially when **defrosting** breads and cakes or baking potatoes. Kitchen paper can also be used to prevent certain foods, such as pastry cases, from drying out too much during cooking. Lightly covering foods, such as bacon rashers, with kitchen paper also prevents splattering in the oven. Plain paper only should be used in the microwave, because the dye in patterned or coloured paper could transfer to the food or oven base during cooking.

kiwi fruit (also called **Chinese gooseberry**) The oval **fruit** of an Asian climbing plant, with hairy skin and bright green flesh. The hairy skin of the kiwi fruit should be removed before eating. They are usually eaten fresh, but they may also be poached in a light syrup or puréed and used in sorbet or ice cream.

kohlrabi The thickened, white stem of a variety of cabbage, whose skin can be white, green or purple and its shape and flavour is similar to turnip. Choose small, firm kohlrabi, trim the top and bottom and peel then slice or dice.

TO COOK: put the kohlrabi into a dish with 2 tbsp of water. Cover the dish and cook 450 g on high for 7–9 minutes, stirring once during cooking. **Stand** for 2 minutes, then drain, season and serve.

kumquat A small, round **citrus fruit** from a Chinese tree, with a bitter-sweet taste. Kumquats can be cooked and used in a sauce for **duck** or made into an orange sauce for ice cream or chocolate desserts.

ladies' fingers   See **okra**.

lamb   The meat of young sheep. All cuts of lamb can be cooked in the microwave, but it is important to note that the more even the shape the more even the cooking. When cooking meat on the bone cover the thinner ends with **foil** halfway through cooking. **Browning agents** may also be used to improve the final appearance of the cooked lamb.

TO COOK: joints, such as shoulder and leg, benefit from extra flavouring, for example spikes of rosemary or slivers of garlic inserted into cuts in the fat before cooking. Place the joint in a **roasting dish** and cover with a split **roasting bag**. Turn it over several times during cooking.

To cook a shoulder, leg or loin with bone, place on a **roasting dish**. For medium meat, cook on high allowing 6–8 minutes per 450 g, for well done cook for 7–9 minutes per 450 g. Boned and rolled joints should be cooked in the same way, but for medium meat allow 9 minutes on high per 450 g, and 10 minutes per 450 g for well done. Halfway through the cooking time drain off any juices, which can be saved and used to make a gravy, and turn the meat over. Once cooked cover the lamb and allow it to **stand** for 15 minutes.

A shoulder of lamb, fillets or riblets can be cubed and cooked in a casserole dish. Add seasonings and stock to taste, cover and cook 450 g of meat on high for 5–7 minutes, then on medium for 20 minutes, stirring twice during cooking. Stand for 10 minutes. Leg of lamb can also be cubed and used for kebabs, which taste even better if the lamb is allowed to **marinate** first. The kebabs should be cooked on a roasting dish, allowing 6–8 minutes per 450 g, and turn over halfway.

Loin chops, chump chops, leg steaks, neck cutlets and noisettes are all tender enough to cook in the microwave. Their finished appearance would be improved if a **browning dish** is used, although it would not matter if they are to be cooked in a sauce.

To cook medium allow 5–6 minutes per 450 g and well done 7–9 minutes. Neck cutlets are usually cut thinner and are smaller than the other cuts so may take slightly less time. To cook 1 chop allow $2\frac{1}{2}$–3 minutes on high; 2 chops, $3\frac{1}{2}$–$4\frac{1}{2}$ minutes on high; 3 chops, $4\frac{1}{2}$–$5\frac{1}{2}$ minutes on high; 4 chops, $5\frac{1}{2}$–$6\frac{1}{2}$ minutes on high. If cooking several chops together arrange them in a circle, ensuring that the thinnest parts point towards the centre. Turn all cuts over halfway through cooking, and once cooked cover and stand for 5 minutes before serving.

Best end of neck is bought as a joint with 6 or 7 cutlets. Two cooked together will form a rack of lamb and serve 6 people. Cut away the top 4 cm of fat and meat from the rib bone and interlock the two joints. Season, cook on a roasting dish allowing 6–7 minutes per 450 g for medium and 7–9 minutes for well done. Cover and stand for 10–15 minutes.

Middle neck and scrag end of neck are best cut up and stewed with other ingredients and stock. Cook on high for 5 minutes then on low for 60–70 minutes per 675 g (1lb). Stand for 10 minutes. See also **brain**; **heart**; **kidney**; **liver**; **sweetbread**.

langoustine See **scampi**.

lasagne A form of **pasta** consisting of sheets about 10–12 cm wide, often with rippled or curly edges and sometimes flavoured with spinach (lasagne verde). The lasagne are layered with meat or vegetable sauce and bechamel sauce, topped with cheese and baked in the microwave.

TO COOK: completely immerse the lasagne sheets in a large bowl of boiling water. Cook uncovered on high allowing 8–10 minutes for 225 g of pasta, stirring once. **Stand** for 5 minutes then drain and assemble. Fresh and pre-cooked lasagne can be used without boiling because they soften in the sauce.

leek A **vegetable** with a slender white bulb, cylindrical stem and broad, flat leaves. Choose firm leeks with crisp undamaged green tops.

Smaller to medium size leeks have a sweet flavour and tender texture. Trim off the roots and coarse tops of the green leaves, fan the leaves open and wash well.

TO COOK: slice evenly, put into a dish and cook 225 g on high for 4 minutes and 450 g for 6–8 minutes, stirring once during cooking. Allow to **stand** for 3–5 minutes before serving

lemon A small, yellow and very acidic citrus **fruit**. Lemons are used for flavouring both sweet and savoury foods and are a traditional garnish for fish. A useful tip for squeezing more juice from a lemon is to cook it on high for 30 seconds.

lemonade A refreshing drink that can be made at home with fresh lemon juice, sugar and water.

TO MAKE: pour 3 tbsp of water into a large jug with the grated rind of 2 lemons and 225 g of granulated sugar. Cook on high for 4 minutes, stirring twice during heating. Then add the juice of 4 lemons, allow to cool and chill. Dilute 50 ml of lemonade with 300 ml of iced water to serve.

lemon curd A rich, soft paste made from lemons, sugar, eggs and butter.

TO COOK: melt 100 g of butter in a large bowl on high for 1 minute. Whisk together 3 eggs,

225 g of sugar, the grated rind of 3 lemons, 120 ml of lemon juice and beat in the butter. Cook uncovered on medium for $2\frac{1}{2}$ minutes, then stir and cook for a further 2–3 minutes until it is thick enough to coat the back of a wooden spoon. Do not boil or the mixture will curdle. Pour at once into sterilized jars and top with discs of waxed paper, cover and seal. Store the curd in the refrigerator for up to three months.

lemon sole See **sole**.

lentil A highly nutritious **pulse**. Red, green and brown lentils all have similar nutritional values and are often referred to as a continental lentil. The orange-coloured lentil is tiny and already skinned and split when purchased. It is more commonly known as the red lentil and has a subtle spicy flavour.

TO COOK: place whole lentils in a sieve and rinse under cold water, removing any grit and stones. Put into a large dish and immerse with fresh, boiling water. Cover the dish and cook 225 g of lentils on high for 20–25 minutes, stirring 2 or 3 times during the cooking. Leave to **stand** for 10–15 minutes and if they are still hard cook for a little longer.

lime A small, round or oval **citrus fruit** with a green skin and distinctive flavour. Limes are used in sweet and savoury dishes and to garnish food.

listeria A type of bacteria commonly found in soil, water and the digestive system of animals. Food sources from which it may enter the human body are unwashed vegetables, some soft cheeses, patés and pre-cooked chilled foods, which may result in the disease listeriosis. Generally, listeria does not harm those who may come into contact with it, but pregnant women, the sick and elderly are at risk, and can become seriously ill because they have less immunity to infection. It can, in severe cases, lead to miscarriage, meningitis and even death.

Listeria is destroyed at temperatures above 70°C. When **reheating** food ensure that the food is thoroughly heated and is piping hot right through to the centre. Only heat 'cook-chill' foods once and never consume after they have passed their sell-by date. When cooking in a microwave it is always important to keep to the stated **standing times**, especially when preparing ready-made meals and always follow the instructions on the packaging. See **food poisoning**.

liver A type of **offal** from lamb, pig, calf, ox and poultry. Liver can be very successfully cooked in the microwave, but timing is critical because it becomes hard and grainy if overdone.

Calf liver is the most expensive and delicately flavoured, and needs only the briefest of cooking. Lamb liver has a slightly stronger flavour. Both types of liver should be bought sliced. Pig liver has a very strong, distinctive flavour and ox liver has a coarser texture, both are best cooked in the microwave in one piece, then braised in a savoury sauce.

TO COOK: remove skin and any tough membranes. Cook in a **browning dish** (that has been pre-heated for 5 minutes) and add a little oil, pressing the liver down into it. Cook 225 g of liver on high for 3–4 minutes and 450 g for 6–7 minutes, turning halfway through the cooking time. Cover and **stand** for 3 minutes.

Pig and ox liver may also be cooked slowly in a sauce for a further 25–30 minutes on medium, until tender. See also **chicken liver**.

loaf dish A loaf-shaped dish made from durable plastic, used to cook cakes, meat loaves and patés in the microwave. See also **cookware**.

lobster Any of various crustacean **shellfish**. The colour of a lobster varies depending on the species. They are bought live and are best cooked conventionally, indeed raw lobster should never be cooked in a microwave. Ready-cooked lobsters should have limbs intact with no discoloration at the joints, the tail should be curled and the eyes bright. Cooked lobster can be made into many delicious dishes that can be cooked in the microwave, such as thermidor.

loganberry   The dark, purplish-red **fruit** of a trailing prickly shrub, resembling a large raspberry. Loganberries are available in midsummer and are used fresh or puréed to make ice cream, sorbet, soufflé, mousse or fruit tarts and pies.

lotus root   A thick, fibrous root with a delicate nutty flavour. Lotus root is usually available dried or canned and is suitable only for use as part of a mixed vegetable dish. Dried lotus roots should be soaked in water overnight before use.

lower power level   A microwave with **variable power control** has low as the minimum power output level, which can be as low as 60 W or as much as 120 W, and the power input will be 10–25%. The lower power level setting is useful for keeping food warm and for the gentle defrosting of large items.

lychee, litchi, lichee or **lichi**   A small Chinese fruit, similar to a **plum**, with dry pink skin and white, sweet flesh. To prepare the fruit, use a small sharp knife to cut the skin, peel back and cut the flesh to remove the stone. Add to fruit salad, savoury salads or use in certain Chinese dishes, especially sweet and sour, chicken, fish and pork dishes.

macaroni or **maccaroni** A type of **pasta** consisting of thick tubes of pasta often broken into 3 cm lengths.

TO COOK: cook macaroni in plenty of water on high for 8 minutes.

mackerel A round, fatty **fish** with blue-black markings and a rich pink flesh, normally sold whole. Choose very fresh mackerel and ask the fishmonger to clean them, but it is still best to wash them again before cooking.

TO COOK: score the whole fish on both sides. Arrange two medium-sized mackerel (approximately 225 g each) on a dish, head to tail, and add 2 tbsp of water. Cover the dish and cook on high for 4 minutes, turning once during cooking. Four fish need 8–10 minutes. Allow to **stand** for 3 minutes.

magnetron A two-electrode electronic valve used with an applied magnetic field to generate high-powered microwave oscillations. In effect it is the part of the microwave oven that converts electricity into microwave energy.

mangetout (also known as **sugar pea**) The immature pod of the garden pea. Before cooking mangetout wash them, top and tail and remove the side strings.

TO COOK: place 225 g of mangetout in a dish, add 2 tbsp of water and cook on high for 3–4 minutes. Drain and serve with a little butter.

mango A tropical **fruit** with sweet, orange-yellow flesh. Choose mangoes with smooth, firm but soft skin and avoid any with wrinkled or blemished skin. Peel the fruit and cut the flesh into slices or cubes and remove the stone. They are most often added to fruit salads and desserts, but they are also used to make chutneys, added to curries and to ice cream.

maple syrup A syrup made from the sap of the maple tree. Maple syrup has a characteristic sweet flavour. It is traditionally served with pancakes, ice cream, waffles and often used in confectionery.

TO WARM: pour into a microwave-safe jug and heat 250–500 ml on high for $1\frac{1}{2}$–2 minutes, until warm.

margarine A butter substitute made from vegetable or animal oils. Margarine can be hard or soft and used for spreading like butter or used for cooking.

marinade A liquid mixture of oil, wine, vinegar and flavourings, such as garlic and herbs, which is used to soak **meat**, **poultry** or **game** before cooking. The marinade will tenderize and flavour the food as well as helping to keep it moist during microwave cooking.

marjoram (also called **sweet marjoram**) The sweet-scented leaves of a Mediterranean plant used as a **herb**. Related to oregano, marjoram has a sweet, slightly spicy flavour, making it a useful, all-purpose herb. Fresh marjoram can be added to salads, omelettes, sauces, meatloaf and chicken casserole.

marmalade A preserve made by boiling the pulp and rind of citrus fruits, especially Seville oranges, with sugar. The skin of the fruit should be cut into thin shreds because large chunks of peel do not soften in the microwave and are unpleasant to eat.

When making marmalade put the pips into a bowl with 300 ml of water and cook on high for 10 minutes. Strain the thick liquid into the cook fruit. This is an easier method than using a muslin bag. See also **jam**.

marrow The large green fruit of a creeping plant with a delicate flavour. Marrow can be peeled, seeded and diced before cooking like courgettes. Those with their seeds removed and cut into slices or halved lengthways make excellent containers for stuffing.

TO COOK: place 450 g of cubed marrow in a dish and add herbs and seasoning to taste. Cover the dish and cook in their own juices for 5–7 minutes on high. Drain, toss in butter and serve.

marzipan A paste made from ground almonds and sugar bound with egg white.

Marzipan is most often used as a cake topping and moulded into cake decorations.

matzo meal A coarse meal ground from matzo (a very thin biscuit of unleavened bread). Matzo meal is used instead of flour in sweet or savoury dishes.

meat The flesh of mammals used for food as distinguished from that of birds and fish. Always bring meat to room temperature before cooking to achieve the best results. If a crisp finish is preferred, cook the meat for half the time in the microwave and the remainder of the time in a conventional oven. Do not salt meat before cooking because this tends to draw out moisture and toughen the outside.

Meat should be raised above its juices when cooking and this is most easily achieved by standing it in a **roasting dish**. The fats and juices must be drained off during cooking because they can make a joint of meat soggy.

Once meat is cooked it has to have a **standing time**. It should be loosely covered with foil and left for 15–20 minutes. The temperature of the meat continues to rise during this period and a **thermometer** should be used to tell when the cooking is completed.

Small or tougher pieces of meat benefit from **marinating** before cooking, or being sprinkled with a meat-tendering powder. Cut the meat into small, thin strips or cubes, because these cook more quickly and evenly than thicker, whole pieces. See also **beef**; **game**; **lamb**; **pork**; **veal**.

Mediterranean prawn (also called **king prawn** or **crevettes**) These are large **prawns** with blue coloured shells, usually sold cooked, but they are also available raw, whole or without heads.

TO COOK: place them in a dish and cover. Cook 225 g for about 2–3 minutes and 450 g for 4–6 minutes until the shells turn pink, and turn them halfway through cooking. Do not overcook or they will toughen.

To reheat cooked prawns, cook with garlic butter 225 g on high for 2 minutes and 450 g for 4 minutes stirring regularly, or until heated completely through. See also **shellfish**.

medium-high power Microwave ovens with **variable power control** have medium-high power, which can be between 450–550 W output level, or numbers 7,8 or 9, depending on the number of variables. It may also be called roast, reheat or sauté, and have a power input of between 70–90%

medium-low power The **variable power control** setting for medium low can be represented by 250 W output, number 3 or 4, or called braise, and have a power input of 40%; on some models this may also be the **defrost** level.

medium power This power level can fall between 300–400 W output or be called simmer or bake; it could also be represented by 50–60% power input. See **variable power control**.

memory control The cooking and timing programme on the control panel can store instructions until required for cooking at a particular power level for a specified amount of time. A delayed start is also offered. These controls are complicated and so need to be studied and used carefully.

meringue A baked mixture of beaten egg whites and sugar, which cannot be cooked in the microwave. An alternative version, however, can be made using firm fondant that will rise and crisp, and be very white.

TO COOK: beat 1 egg white lightly and gradually work in 375–400 g of sifted icing sugar, forming a dry, firm fondant. Divide the mixture into small (2 cm) balls and arrange a dozen at a time in two circles on greaseproof paper or non-stick parchment in the oven. Cook on high for $1\frac{1}{4}$–$1\frac{1}{2}$ minutes or until the meringues are puffed up and set. Allow to cool.

microwave cookware   See **cookware**.

microwave oven   An oven in which food is cooked by microwaves. Perhaps the most useful cooking appliance developed in recent years. It can be used just as effectively and efficiently by a family or a single person. Microwave ovens work more quickly than conventional fuel ovens and use far less energy. Microwave cooking takes, very approximately, about one-third of conventional cooking times, but this depends on the density of the food, its starting temperature (frozen, refrigerated or room) and the quantity being cooked.

Cooking with microwaves reduces smells and cuts down on oven cleaning because foods do not get burned onto the cooker's surface. Foods retain their nutrients, texture, shape, colour and flavour because they are cooked quickly and do not require large quantities of water.

Microwaving is particularly good for **defrosting** and **reheating**, which can often be carried out in minutes. See also **care of the microwave**; **cleaning a microwave oven**; **faults in a microwave oven**; **features of the microwave oven**; **safety of the microwave**; **variable power control**; **wattage**.

microwave tool   A utensil specifically designed for use in the microwave. Microwave tools may include bent-handled tools, such as a ladle or a spoon. Made from plastic they can be left in the bowl for stirring during cooking.

milk The whitish, nutritious fluid produced by mature, female mammals. The most popular milk consumed is cows' milk, although ewes' milk and goats' milk are also available. There are a range of milk varieties, according to the fat content, from the rich Channel Island milk to whole milk (with a fat content of 3.9 g/100 ml), semi-skimmed (1.7 g/100 ml) and skimmed (0.1 g/100 ml). Most milk undergoes some form of heat treatment (pasteurization) to destroy bacteria and to improve its keeping qualities.

When buying milk check the use-by date and the conditions of the packaging. Milk purchased in bottles and plastic containers should not be left exposed to light. Store covered, away from strong smelling foods. Serve or use straight from the refrigerator. Use in drinks, soups, sauces, and desserts.

To scald milk, pour 250 ml into a microwave-safe jug. Heat on high for 2–2½ minutes until bubbles form around the edge.

milk pudding A hot or cold pudding made by boiling or baking milk with a grain, especially rice. These are set during cooking by the action of the eggs or by adding rennet. Various ingredients and flavourings are added to give a wide range of desserts. Care must be taken not to overcook milk puddings containing eggs, otherwise they coagulate and curdle. Baked-custard is probably the most popular milk pudding, with crème brûlée being a richer version made with cream. See also **rice pudding**; **sago**; **semolina**; **tapioca**.

millet The seeds of a hardy annual grass, which can be bought in the form of grains, flakes and flour, and is gluten free. The grains can be cooked and made into pilaf and added to burgers, the flakes can be cooked to make a creamy porridge.

TO COOK: place 50 g of millet in a bowl. Add 300 ml of boiling water, cover and cook on high for 12–15 minutes, stirring twice. **Stand** for 4 minutes and drain if necessary.

mince Ground meat, most commonly **beef**, but it may also be **lamb**, **pork** or **veal**. Mince cooks well in the microwave and is useful for quick dishes, sauces (bolognaise) making burgers, meat balls, meat loaves, patties and stuffings for vegetables.

mince pie A small pastry tart filled with mincemeat. Reheat six ready-made mince pies at one time on medium (50%) for $1\frac{1}{2}$ minutes. **Stand** for 1–2 minutes before eating. It is important to remember to remove bought mince pies from **foil** containers. Also be careful if reheating home-made mince pies that contain a lot of **alcohol** or brandy.

mint The aromatic leaves of a temperate shrub used as a **herb**. Mint is one of the most important and widely used of herbs, there are many varieties including apple mint, spearmint and ginger mint. It is a traditional flavouring for peas and new potatoes and is chopped to make a mint sauce to accompany lamb.

mixed spice A mixture of sweet-flavoured, ground **spices**. Mixed spice is used mostly in sweet dishes, cakes, biscuits and confectionery. It consists of cloves, allspice, cinnamon, nutmeg and ginger.

monkfish A round, white fish with a very large, ugly head. Like all white fish, monkfish cooks extremely well in the microwave. It has firm-textured flesh with a delicate flavour. It is sold without the head and may be referred to as monkfish tails and sold as fillets. Trim off any loose membranes and wash. Monkfish can be cooked in one piece, cut into steaks or cubed and made into kebabs.
 TO COOK: put into a dish, brush with butter or sprinkle with wine, cover and cook 225 g on high for 2–3 minutes, turning once. **Stand** for 5 minutes.

mousse A light, creamy dessert made with whisked eggs and cream and variously flavoured. Mousses may be served hot or chilled. They are usually flavoured with fruit, chocolate, nuts, coffee, a liqueur or spirits.

muffin tray See **deep bun dish**.

mullet (red and grey) A small white fish of two distinct varieties. Grey mullet is silvery in colour with firm white flesh and sold whole or in fillets. Red mullet is smaller, crimson in colour with a delicate flavour and sold whole (the liver is usually left inside and considered a delicacy). As with all round fish, the skin should be slashed two or three times on each side before cooking.

TO COOK: place the fish in a buttered dish, season with fennel and white wine. Cover the dish and cook on high, allowing about 4 minutes per 450 g or a little longer for grey mullet. **Stand** for 5 minutes.

mung bean A small, dark green **pulse**, used whole or skinned and split. Mung beans have a mild flavour when cooked and they are most widely used for sprouting. After soaking them rinse and drain.

TO COOK: put the beans into a large bowl and immerse with boiling water. Cover the dish and cook 225 g on high for 20–25 minutes, stirring 2 or 3 times during cooking. Leave to **stand** for about 10 minutes.

mushroom Any of a variety of edible fungi, the commonest being the field mushroom. Whole or sliced mushrooms cooked in the microwave have a good texture and flavour. The best mushrooms should be fresh and firm. Before using them wipe with a damp cloth and trim off the stalks.

TO COOK: place 100 g of mushrooms in a bowl and dot with butter. Cook on high for $1\frac{1}{2}$–2 minutes, stirring once during cooking. **Stand** for 1 minute.

mussel A mollusc **shellfish**. Mussels, like all live shellfish, must be absolutely fresh and should be eaten the day they are bought. Scrub the shells to remove any grit, scrape off the barnacles with a sharp knife and pull away the beards. Wash them in plenty of cold water and discard any mussels with broken or cracked shells or any that have open shells that do not close when tapped.

TO COOK: place 1 kg of mussels in a large bowl with some white wine. Cover the dish and cook on high for 4–5 minutes, stirring twice during cooking. Allow to **stand** for 3 minutes and discard any whose shells are still closed.

mustard A hot condiment made with the powdered seeds of the mustard plant. White, brown and black mustard seeds are used in curries and Indian dishes. Mustard powder is a mixture of mustard varieties mixed with wheat flour and turmeric. Added to cheese dishes it brings out the flavour. Many types of prepared mustard are available often with interesting additions of fresh herbs and green peppercorns. Dijon mustard is one of the most popular types and an essential ingredient in salad dressings.

mutton The meat of a mature sheep. Mutton is tougher than **lamb** and is traditionally stewed to tenderize it. It is not readily available and is not recommended for microwave cooking.

nectarine A soft, juicy, smooth-skinned **fruit**, which is a variety of **peach**.

TO COOK: place 225 g of prepared fruit in a dish and add 600 ml of syrup or fruit juice. Cover the dish and cook on high for 2–3 minutes, stirring once during cooking. **Stand** for 3 minutes. Poached nectarines are delicious served with a purée of raspberries.

noodle A ribbon-like strip of **pasta**. There are many varieties of egg noodle available and are best known for their use in Chinese cookery. They can be bought fresh, coiled in circles or, when dried, in flat rectangular cakes. Made from a dough of wheat flour and eggs, they may vary in thickness from fine to thick strands. Noodles can be used for soups, stir-fries (after they have been cooked) or as an accompaniment.

TO COOK: place 225 g of egg noodles in a bowl and cover with boiling water. Stir then cook on high for 2–4 minutes, stirring once during cooking. **Stand** for 3 minutes then drain.

Rice noodles are sold as long strands and also known as rice sticks, transparent or cellophane rice noodles and all come in varying thicknesses. They need to be soaked before cooking and are added to soups or stir-fries.

nutmeg The hard, aromatic seed of an evergreen tree, used as a **spice** when finely grated.

Whole nutmegs should be sound and unbroken. Ground nutmeg is unevenly coloured dark brown and highly aromatic. It is used to flavour milk puddings, cakes, biscuits, soups, bread and beverages made with milk. Nutmeg also enhances mushroom, spinach and cabbage dishes. Mace is the lace covering surrounding the nutmeg kernel and is used in its dried form. A blade of mace is a useful flavouring for white sauce.

nuts The edible kernel of various hard, woody fruits of certain trees. The microwave is useful for toasting nuts to be used as toppings, fillings and to decorate sweet dishes. To roast nuts, spread 100 g of shelled nuts on a plate, and cook uncovered on high for 2–3 minutes until lightly browned, stirring 2–3 times. Whole nuts take a little longer than chopped nuts.

To make savoury nuts add spices and seasonings before cooking. When cool serve as a snack or as an addition to salads.

To blanch nuts, see **almond**. See **brazil nut**; **cashew nut**; **chestnut**; **hazelnut**; **peanut**; **pecan nut**; **pistachio nut**; **walnut**.

oat A cereal used mainly for making groats, rolled oats, flakes, bran, oatmeal and flour. Oat flakes are made by flattening the oat grain and used as a main ingredient in muesli, and also in biscuits and bread.

Oatmeal is tiny flakes of oat grain sometimes milled until very fine and used for breakfast cereals, pancakes, muffins, bread, oatcakes and biscuits. Rolled oats are flattened flakes of grain and they are used to make **porridge**, for muesli, biscuits and savoury mixtures such as rissoles.

octopus A soft-bodied mollusc with eight tentacled legs. Available in varying sizes, but small octopus are the best for cooking. Choose octopus with firm flesh and a pleasant sea smell. By the time it gets to the fishmonger the baggy head with innards have been removed. With any recipe used the octopus requires preliminary cooking.

TO COOK: place in a large glass dish, but do not add any water or seasonings. Cover the dish and cook on medium for 40–45 minutes. The octopus will exude a dark red liquid when it is pierced with a pointed knife. When cooked rinse it under cold water and discard the liquid. The fine skin and knobby bosses can be rubbed off easily. Put the pinkish, white star of tentacles into a dish with flavouring and 4 tbsp of water. Cover the dish and cook on high for 4–5 minutes. Then drain and serve with a sauce or allow to cool and add to seafood salad.

offal A general name to include everything that is removed when dressing the meat carcass. In culinary terms it refers to **heart**, **liver**, **kidney**, **brain**, **tripe**, **tongue**, **oxtail** and **sweetbreads**. With careful cooking it can be tender as well as tasty and nutritious.

oil Liquid, edible fats that are commonly extracted from seeds and nuts. Common sources of vegetable oils include sesame seeds, olives, sunflower seeds, rapeseed and walnuts. Most vegetable oils are unsaturated or polyunsaturated, with the exception of coconut and palm oil, which are saturated.

Some of the most widely used cooking oils include **corn oil**, **olive oil**, groundnut (peanut) oil, **safflower oil**, **sunflower oil**, **rapeseed oil** and soya bean oil. To extract their oil, seeds and fruits are first pressed by pressure alone to extract the maximum oil; this is known as cold-pressed oil and is the best quality available. To extract more oil the pulp is then heated and other chemicals may be added in later pressings. Antioxidants may also be added to increase the keeping qualities.

Vegetable oil is a mixture of oils extracted from seeds or fruit and can vary significantly in quality, colour and flavour. Most oils are sensitive to heat and light and deteriorate on storage. Store in a clean, sealed container, at or below room temperature and away from direct light. Salad oils may be stored in the refrigerator, but other oils solidify at lower temperatures. Liquid oils are used for general cooking purposes and salad oils. When cooking in the microwave, less oil or fat is generally needed compared to conventional cooking methods.

okra (also known as **ladies' fingers**) The long, tapering, green seed pod of an African and Asian plant, which has juicy green flesh and thick gluey sap. Wash and dry the okra and trim off the stalks, but do not cut into the pod if cooking whole. They can be sliced or left whole, added to stews and are an essential ingredient for gumbo.

TO COOK: put 225 g of whole okra in a dish with 4 tbsp of water. Cover the dish and cook on high for 4–5 minutes until tender, but still quite firm, stirring once during cooking. Drain and serve with curries and spiced rice dishes.

olive oil A pale yellow, greenish oil pressed from the pulp of ripe olive fruits. Olive oil has a characteristic pleasant, fruity odour and flavour. Its colour may vary depending on the region in which the olive is grown, and from pale to dark depending on the type of oil. After the first pressing to give cold-pressed oil the pulp is pressed again to yield 'virgin' oil. This has not been chemically treated and there are several grades of virgin oil. Each successive pressing yields oil of a lower grade, which must generally be refined to improve its flavour and storage life. Pure olive oil is a blend of virgin and refined oils.

onion A bulb with a pungent odour and taste. Onions are available in many varieties, ranging in colour from white and yellow to shades of purple and red; and in size from minute ones (commonly used for pickling) to the large, mild Spanish variety. Onions also vary in strength of flavour and even individual varieties can change as the growing season progresses, developing from mild to strong, or vice versa. It is best to choose firm onions with dry papery skins, do not use any that are softening or sprouting. The microwave oven softens them quickly and contains their smell. When adding to other dishes they are best chopped rather than sliced.

TO COOK: put 225 g of chopped onions into a bowl with either 2 tbsp of water or 1 tbsp of oil. Cover the bowl and cook on high for 2–4 minutes, stirring once during cooking. For whole, stuffed onions, cook them uncovered on high for 4–8 minutes depending on the size of the onions used. Turn them around halfway through cooking and allow to **stand** for 3 minutes.

onion soup mix A commercially prepared mixture, which can be sprinkled on meats or beefburger to help brown the surface during cooking.

orange A **citrus fruit**, with three main varieties: the thick-skinned navel; the sweet Valencia; and the bitter Seville. The Seville orange is the preferred variety for making **marmalade**. Segments of orange can be added to salad, made into a sauce to accompany duck, ham, chicken and veal or used in a variety or desserts.

A useful tip for squeezing more juice from an orange is to heat it on high for 30 seconds.

oregano The pungent leaves of a Mediterranean variety of **marjoram**, which are dried and used chopped as a **herb**. Oregano is widely used in Italian cookery, such as pizza and pasta, and gives character to any tomato dish. To dry oregano in the microwave, place it on kitchen paper and cook on high for 25 seconds.

ovenproof glass **Cookware** made of heatproof glass can be used in the microwave for cooking and heating as long as they have no metal trim or content. Special microwave-safe glass is available for cooking at high temperatures, such as in jam making.

oxtail The skinned tail of an ox, a type of **offal** used to make soup and stew. Oxtail is usually sold cut up into 5 cm pieces. It needs very long, slow cooking in liquid to tenderize it and is best made the day before serving. Refrigerate the dish so that the fat sets on the surface and can then be removed.

TO COOK: cook 1 kg of oxtail in a **browning dish** (pre-heated for 5 minutes), press the tail down and cook on high for 6–8 minutes. Transfer to a dish and add onions, carrots, celery and stock. Cover the dish and cook on medium for about 1 hour or until tender, stirring during cooking. **Stand** for 10 minutes.

oysters   A mollusc **shellfish** usually eaten raw. The shells are mostly grey-black in colour. Oysters are usually bought raw, intact in their shell. When opened the oysters should be a natural creamy-grey colour, shiny and fresh-smelling with clear liquid. They should not be cooked in a microwave.

palm heart The delicately flavoured bud of a cabbage palm plant. Fresh palm hearts are usually eaten cooked and with melted butter or cold with mayonnaise. Choose crisp, clean, conical shaped palm hearts about 15 cm long. Canned ones can be served similarly.

TO COOK: wash fresh palm hearts thoroughly. Peel off the outer skin and cut into short lengths if necessary, and put into a dish with 4 tbsp of water. Cover the dish and cook 225 g on high for 5–6 minutes, 450 g for 7–9 minutes. Cooking time will vary depending on the thickness of the hearts.

pancake A flat cake made from a batter. Pancakes should be cooked conventionally, but the microwave can be used to prepare fillings and for reheating prepared or filled pancakes.

pan frying It is not possible to shallow or deep fry in a microwave cooker and these methods should never be attempted. The large amounts of oil used in frying are very dangerous in a microwave. Using a **browning dish** can achieve a similar result.

papaya (also called **pawpaw**) A pear-shaped tropical **fruit** with smooth yellow skin and orange flesh, similar in taste and texture to a small **melon**. Select undamaged fruit with a sweet perfume and avoid any with damp, dark spots on the skin.

Peel and cut the papaya in half lengthways, scoop out the seeds and slice or dice. Use in fruit salad, cakes, savoury salads, as a marinade to tenderize meat or with chicken or pork dishes. Papayas may also be halved and stuffed and cooked with a savoury filling. Green, unripe papayas may be cooked and used like **marrows**.

paper Plates and dishes made from paper can be used for reheating or cooking in a microwave. However, if food is too wet the paper will go soggy and if too dry the paper sticks to the food. Waxed paper and cardboard can only be used for thawing, otherwise the wax melts from the heat of the food. Paper napkins and absorbent **kitchen paper** are ideal for mopping up fat or preventing splattering. See also **greaseproof paper**.

paprika A sweet mild powder made from a variety of red pepper. A useful **spice** for its subtle peppery taste. Paprika's colour means that it can be used as a **browning agent**, especially with poultry.

Parmesan or Parmesan cheese A hard, dry cheese made from skimmed milk. Parmesan is best when bought fresh and then grated when required. It is usually added to pasta dishes or sauces.

parsley A small herbaceous European plant used as a **herb**. Parsley is one of the most commonly used herbs. It has a fresh mild flavour and has many uses in cooking, in sauces, stuffings, salads and garnishes, as well as being an important part of a **bouquet garni**. To dry parsley in the microwave, place it on **kitchen paper** and cook on high for 25 seconds.

parsnip A root **vegetable** with white flesh and a distinctive, sweet flavour. The best parsnips should be clean, firm, unblemished and small to medium in size. Wash them, trim off the top and bottom and peel. If the parsnips are to be puréed, cut into cubes, otherwise they can be cooked whole or cut into round slices, segments or **julienne** strips. When cooking halves, arrange with the thinner ends towards the centre.

TO COOK: put 450 g of prepared parsnips into a dish with 2 tbsp of water, 1 tsp of lemon juice and a knob of butter. Cover the dish and cook for 8–10 minutes, stir or rearrange halfway through cooking. Allow to **stand** for 2–3 minutes, drain and toss in more butter before serving.

partridge A small **game** bird. Allow one bird per serving and put a knob of butter in the body cavity, truss it and tie with a strip of bacon over the breast.

TO COOK: for 2 partridges, put the birds in a large **roasting bag** and place them breast-side down in a **roasting dish**. Slit the bag to allow the juices to drain away and cook on medium, allowing 8 minutes per 1lb. Allow to **stand** for 5 minutes.

pasta A dough traditionally made from refined white wheat flour or semolina (durum flour) and water (and sometimes eggs and milk). Pasta is moulded into a number of characteristic shapes and sizes, e.g. **spaghetti**, **lasagne**, **tagliatelle**, **macaroni** and **cannelloni**. Wholemeal pasta has a grainy texture and is brown in colour. Pasta may also be dyed a variety of colours with vegetable purées. It can be bought dried or, increasingly, fresh.

Good quality dried pasta should feel hard and smooth and when cooked should have a wheaty flavour. Fresh pasta should smell fresh and look bright; store in the refrigerator.

Fresh or dried pasta needs no preparation before cooking and generally takes the same time in the microwave as normal cooking.

TO COOK: pour enough boiling water into a dish to immerse the pasta. Add 1 tbsp of oil and a little salt. Cook uncovered, allowing 6–8 minutes for 225 g of dried pasta. **Stand** for 5 minutes and then drain. Fresh pasta takes less time to cook, so heat on high for 1–2 minutes. See also **noodles**.

pastry A dough of flour, water and shortening, which may include eggs, sugar or cheese. Most types of pastry can be cooked in the microwave, but it is better in taste, texture and colour when cooked conventionally. Shortcrust pastry cases must be baked blind before being filled. Cover with absorbent kitchen paper and a plate or use ceramic **baking beans** to keep it fairly crisp; allow for shrinkage. Puff pastry pales and lacks flavour and it is not recommended for cooking in the microwave, but it does cook very well in **combination ovens**. Suet pastry works well for recipes requiring moist heat, such as roly-poly or a suet pudding, but extra raising agent must be added to the recipe.

paté A spread of finely minced meat, poultry, offal, fish or vegetable matter.

Line a loaf dish with microwave **clingfilm** and when cooking elevate the dish on a trivet or rack or on a ramekin turned upside down. Patés can be served as a starter or as a cold dish on a buffet or picnic.

pawpaw See **papaya**.

pea A general name for the seed of certain **pulses**, including the chickpea and the garden pea. The name is commonly applied to the small, characteristically bright green seed of the garden pea, which is eaten cooked as a vegetable. Choose shiny, bright green, well-filled, undamaged pods. If the raw pea tastes sweet, it will still taste sweet when cooked. Shell or 'pod' the vegetable just before use, 450–675 g will yield 225 g of prepared peas.

TO COOK: spread out 225 g of podded peas in a shallow dish and add 2 tbsp of water. Cover the dish and cook on high for 3–4 minutes, stirring during cooking. Allow to **stand** for 3 minutes.

Petit pois, a smaller, tender, sweeter variety, take less time to cook, approximately 2–3 minutes.

peach A reddish-yellow, downy skinned **fruit** with sweet, orange-yellow flesh. Peaches are available in late spring and summer. Choose peaches that are firm, but yield when pressed gently – this indicates ripeness. Wash and dry and serve fresh or use halved, quartered or in segments in fruit or savoury salads. They can also be poached in syrup or served stuffed, or used to make jam, chutney or ice cream.

To make it easier to peel whole peaches, put 4 peaches into a bowl, pour over boiling water and heat on high for 30 seconds until their skins split. Then put them into cold water and remove the skins.

TO COOK: place 225 g of prepared fruit in a dish and add 600 ml of syrup or fruit juice. Cover the dish and cook on high for 2–3 minutes, stirring once during cooking. **Stand** for 3 minutes. Poached peaches are delicious served with a purée of raspberries.

peanut (also called **groundnut** or **monkey nut**) The seed (not in fact a nut) of a small bush that pushes its thin, woody fruit capsules below ground as they mature. Peanuts are available all year round. Buy peanuts in their shells if required to store for a long time. Otherwise buy shelled raw peanuts, roasted or salted in air-tight packages. Remove the skin by pressing the peanut between fingers. Use nuts in salads, with meat, poultry, rice and pasta, biscuits, cakes and ice cream.

peanut butter Roasted ground peanuts, to which some salt is added. When crushed the nuts release an oil which makes them spreadable.

pear A rounded or elongated bell-shaped fruit with thin yellow, green or pinkish skin and juicy, sweet, white flesh with a grainy texture. Choose slightly underripe fruit because once ripe pears deteriorate quickly. These are best poached in a sugar syrup. Most pears have a delicate flavour and benefit from being cooked in cider or wine and sugar rather than water. Peeled pears can be halved and cored, but leave in acidulated water (water with lemon juice added) until ready to cook so they will not discolour.

TO COOK: pour 300 ml of cider or red wine into a dish, add 100 g of sugar and cook on high for 5 minutes, stirring once. Arrange prepared pears in the syrup with the narrow ends towards the centre. Cook on high, allowing 3–4 minutes for 225 g and 5–7 minutes for 450 g, turning them over halfway through cooking. The timings depend on the ripeness of the pears. Allow to cool in the syrup.

pearl barley Barley grains ground and polished. Pearl barley is used to make barley water or added to soups and stews to thicken and enrich them. It may be used in the same way as rice.

TO COOK: put 225 g of pearl barley into a bowl with 750 ml of stock. Cook on high for 25–28 minutes, stirring twice during cooking. Allow to **stand** for 3–5 minutes.

pecan nut The smooth, dark red nut of the pecan tree. The slightly bitter, oily kernel, which looks and tastes like a walnut, is used whole, chopped or ground. Whole nuts may be used in pecan pie, biscuits, fruit cake and tea-bread. Chopped pecans can be used in biscuits and cakes and served with ice cream.

peppercorn The dried fruit of a tropical climbing vine. Peppercorns are used whole or powdered as a **spice**. The unripe fruit is green, turning greenish yellow then red as it ripens. Green peppercorns are included in some special dishes for their colour as much as their flavour. Black pepper is made from peppercorns picked before they are quite ripe and dried in the sun, where they blacken in a day or two. White pepper is made from ripened peppercorns that have been soaked and rubbed to remove their husks. White peppercorns have a sharper, more astringent flavour than black, which can be useful in some dishes. White pepper is often used to season pale dishes and sauces which would be discoloured by flecks of black. Although available ready ground, for the best results, always freshly grind white or black peppercorns.

peppers (also called **pimientos** or **sweet peppers**) A species of capsicum with green (unripe), red, yellow or orange fruits. Peppers are useful both raw in salads, as part of a crudités selection and cooked in casseroles, stir-fries, vegetable mixtures and are good with a savoury filling. Choose peppers with firm glossy skins and do not use any dull wrinkled ones. The colour denotes the degree of ripeness the red being the ripest and sweetest.

To prepare peppers, cut a thin slice off the stalk end. Remove the seeds, rinsing out the inside. Cut into rings, strips or dice, or cut off the tops, scoop out the seeds and stuff.

TO COOK: place rings, slices or halves in a dish, add 1 tbsp of water or hot oil and cook 225 g on high for 2 minutes, stirring once during cooking.

persimmon A large, orange-red tropical **fruit**, similar to a large tomato, with tough, sweet and sharp orange flesh. Persimmon should be left until soft and pulpy before eating, otherwise it is too astringent to eat.

Sharon persimmon is a sweet-tasting variety, with orange skin, developed for eating – skin, seeds and all. It can be used in fruit salad, as a purée for a sauce, or served with cold chicken and meat. It can also be poached in wine or used in pies, cakes and jam.

petit pois See **pea**.

pheasant A popular, seasonal, long-tailed **game** bird. Pheasant is usually cooked by roasting, or in pies and patés. Choose a young bird for roasting because older ones are likely to be tough. If bought ready prepared the bird will have been hung to give them their gamey flavour. They are usually bought as a brace (pair), but can be bought singly. The hen is plumper and more tender than the cock and is generally considered to have a better flavour. Tie some fat over the breast, or cover with slices of streaky bacon before cooking.

TO COOK: place a knob of butter in the body cavity of a 900 g pheasant. Put the bird breast-side down in a **roasting dish** and cover with a slit or pierced **roasting bag**. Cook on medium for 7–8 minutes per lb and turn over halfway through cooking. Protect any parts that over-cook with small pieces of **foil**. Cover and **stand** for 5 minutes.

piercing A build up of steam can occur during cooking so any foods with a tight fitting skin or membrane, such as raw egg yolk, chicken livers, whole fruit or vegetables, must be pierced before cooking to prevent them exploding. Rather than pierce whole fish, slash on both sides at the thickest part. This also helps to cook them more evenly.

pigeon A small **game** bird, usually cooked by braising, roasting or served in pies. Young pigeon can be cooked in the microwave and like all game birds needs a covering of fat or bacon before cooking.

TO COOK: for 2 pigeons, put the birds in a large **roasting bag** and place them breast-side down in a **roasting dish**. Slit the bag to allow the juices to drain away and cook on medium, allowing 8 minutes per lb. Allow to **stand** for 5 minutes.

pilchard A small, oily **fish** of the herring family, usually eaten fresh or canned in oil or tomato sauce. See **sardine**.

pimiento See **peppers**.

pineapple A large tropical fruit with tough skin and fibrous, juicy, yellow flesh. Choose a pineapple that is plump and heavy in relation to its size with fresh-looking skin and fresh green leaves. Cut the leaves off and slice off the bottom. Stand the fruit upright and slice all the skin off, cutting downwards, then remove all eyes with a sharp knife. Slice into rings and remove the core; or cut the pineapple in half lengthways and cut out the core before cutting into wedges or cubes. Add to microwave fruit salads, tarts, savoury salads and sweet and sour Chinese dishes, serve with ham or chicken, or chop and use in cakes and pies.

pine kernel (also known as **pine nut**) The oily, aromatic seed of certain varieties of pine tree, it is a small, cream-coloured, soft kernel. Pine kernels may be roasted, dry fried or left plain for a more delicate flavour. Add pine kernels to stuffings, pasta sauce, lamb, game, salads, savoury vegetable dishes, cakes, biscuits and fruit salad.

pistachio nut A small, hard-shelled nut with a green kernel, related to the cashew nut. Pistachio nuts may be eaten fresh or roasted or used to flavour foods such as ice cream. They may also be used in patés and terrines, desserts, confectionery and for decorating cakes and cold soufflés. To remove their skins blanch them as with **almonds**.

pitta bread A flat, rounded, unleavened bread. Pitta may be made with refined white or wholemeal flour and may have seasonings or garlic added.

TO HEAT: wrap 2 pitta bread individually in **kitchen paper**, place on a paper plate or directly in the oven. Cook on high for 12–17 seconds (1 pitta bread 10–15 seconds) until the bread is warm.

pizza A disc of dough usually topped with tomatoes, cheese and a variety of other ingredients. Pizzas can be cooked in the microwave, but the dough base will not be hard. This can be overcome, however, by cooking them in a **browning dish** or a griddle, though the top edges will still not have a crusty finish.

plaice A white flatfish with brown skin, red or orange spots and a mild flavour. Plaice may be bought whole or in fillets. The fillets can be poached like **flounder** or cooked in a **browning dish** (pre-heated for 5 minutes).

TO COOK: place 225 g of fillets in a dish in a single layer, if possible, and season to taste. Cover the dish tightly and cook on high for 2–3 minutes.

plantain A variety of large banana, which is cooked and eaten when green. Raw plantain is indigestible and must be cooked. It is excellent when added to curry, casseroles or made into a soup. It may also be peeled, sliced and cooked, and served as an accompaniment to meat dishes. Choose firm, undamaged fruit and store at room temperature.

TO COOK: melt 25 g of butter in a dish and add 225 g of sliced plantain. Cover the dish and cook on high for 3–4 minutes until tender, stirring halfway through cooking.

plastic A synthetic material that is used to make the majority of microwave **cookware**. Plastic is both dishwasher safe and designed to withstand high temperatures. Lightweight plastic containers, such as yoghurt pots, may also be used in the microwave for defrosting, but they are liable to melt and distort when the food becomes hot. Plastic microwave boiling bags and **roasting bags** also make good containers. Ordinary plastic bags should not be used because they are not able to withstand the heat. See also **microwave tools**.

plated meals Leftovers can be reheated in the microwave placed on a plate. All the food must be of the same temperature, either chilled or at room temperature. Arrange the food so that thicker, denser food, such as pieces of meat, are placed on the outside of the plate with the more quickly heated foods, such as vegetables, on the inside. Delicate foods should be placed underneath denser meat slices to avoid overcooking them. Cover the plate with microwave-safe **clingfilm** and reheat until piping hot, rotating the plate as often as possible. To reheat a complete meal of meat, gravy, potatoes and vegetables, cover the plate with clingfilm and cook on defrost for 5 minutes. Allow the food to **stand** for 2 minutes and then cook on high for 2 minutes. See also **stacking ring**.

plum A small, thin-skinned fruit that may be purple, green or yellow and with sweet yellow or pinkish flesh. Plums are available in late summer and autumn, and the best ones should be plump, fully coloured and undamaged. Wash and serve them raw, or purée and use for sauces, sorbet, ice cream and desserts. Poached plums can be used in pies, tarts, cakes and puddings.

TO COOK: halve the fruit and remove the stones. Place into a dish with a little sugar and 2 tbsp of water or red wine. Cover the dish and cook 225 g of plums on high for 3 minutes and 450 g for 5 minutes, stirring once during cooking. Allow to **stand** for 5 minutes.

poaching A method of cooking food by simmering it very gently. Fish, chicken, vegetables and fruits may all be successfully poached in the microwave. The foods are poached in very little liquid, usually much less than when cooked conventionally, because the food cooks in its own moisture.

polenta A yellow-white, coarse, granular flour made from corn or maize. Polenta is made by mixing maize with water and a little salt, and then cooked to make a very thick porridge. It is traditionally shaped into a large flat loaf and cut into thick slices. It is used in stews or fried in oil or bacon fat and served with a rich tomato sauce.

TO COOK: pour 600 ml of boiling water or stock onto 100 g of polenta and mix until smooth. Cook on high for 5–8 minutes until very thick, stirring occasionally. Add 25 g of butter or margarine and seasoning. Spoon into a greased shallow dish and **stand** for 10–15 minutes.

pomegranate A round tropical **fruit** with a hard reddish skin and pink flesh containing many small seeds. Select large pomegranates with shiny red skins and avoid shrivelled ones.

To eat or prepare, cut open the skin and scoop out the seeds in their sacs of pulp and discard the bitter membrane. Use in fruit salad, sauces, with chicken, fish and Turkish dishes. Pomegranate juice can be used in drinks, sweet soups, sauces, sorbets or jellies.

popcorn The edible kernels of a variety of maize, which swell up and burst when heated, exposing the light, puffy centre of the grain. A popcorn in-the-bag product is available for use in the microwave. Follow the manufacturer's instructions on the pack carefully and never 'pop' corn in the microwave using any other bag than the one provided because it may catch fire.

poppadom A thin, round, crisp Indian bread, which is roasted or fried and served with Indian dishes.

TO COOK: brush the poppadoms lightly with oil on both sides and place them on **kitchen paper** on the oven floor. Heat on full for 1 minute or until crisp, turning once.

poppy seed The small grey to black seeds of a certain variety of poppy. Poppy seeds have a pleasant nutty flavour and are used to decorate bread and desserts and sprinkled over salads and pasta.

pork Pig **meat**. The lean of pork should be pale pink and finely grained with white, firm fat. It should have no smell. Pork is a meat that must be well cooked without a trace of pink left in the centre. A large piece of pork can be cooked in the microwave. However, even oiling and salting the rind does not produce the crisp crackling of a conventional roast.

For the best results choose a joint that is the same thickness throughout so that it cooks more evenly. If this is not possible, **shield** the thinner areas with small pieces of **foil**.

TO COOK: joints of pork, such as loin and leg, should have a little oil and salt rubbed into the scored skin. Stand the meat in a **roasting dish** and cover with a slit **roasting bag** or a piece of **greaseproof paper**. Cook on high allowing 9–10 minutes per 450 g, turn over halfway through the cooking time and allow to **stand** for 15–20 minutes. For boned and rolled joints, including the shoulder joint, cook for 10–12 minutes per 450 g and also allow to stand for 15–20 minutes. An apple sauce can be made in the microwave while the joint is standing.

Check that the meat is cooked by using a **thermometer**. Before leaving the joint to stand it should read 75°C (165°F) and then rise to

85°C (185°F) during the standing time.

Other cuts of pork that can be cooked as a joint include the blade, which will be boned and rolled and may be stuffed. Cook this for 17–20 minutes per 450 g, or 21–25 minutes if stuffed.

Pork loin chops, usually 1.5 cm thick, are best cooked on a pre-heated **browning dish** to colour them. Arrange with the narrow ends towards the centre and cook 2, 175 g chops for 4 minutes, turning them over halfway. Sparerib chops need a little longer. After the cooking time cover the chops and allow them to stand for 5 minutes.

A sparerib joint is best **braised**. Place the joint in a dish with 8 tbsp of dry cider or stock and add seasoning. Cover the dish and for each 450 g of meat allow 15 minutes, the first 6–8 minutes on high and the remainder of the time on medium, turning the joint over halfway. Leave the joint to stand for 20 minutes.

Spareribs are usually cut into single rib pieces and improve when marinated. Place in a dish and allow 10 minutes per 450 g. Cook them on high for the first 5 minutes, then drain off the fat, turn the ribs over and brush with marinade or barbecue sauce and continue to cook on medium. Stand for 5 minutes.

Tenderloin, also known as pork fillet, is a tender cut and can be cooked whole, cut into chunks or flattened out into escalopes. To cook a piece of fillet cut a pocket the length of the fillet and stuff with a well-seasoned mixture. Tie with string and shield the thin ends with foil. Place the meat onto a roasting rack and then put it on a dish. Cook on high for 5 minutes then on medium for 10–12 minutes per 450 g. Remove the foil and turn the fillet over halfway. Cover and allow to stand for 10 minutes. See also **bacon**; **gammon**; **sausages**.

porridge A smooth paste made with oats cooked in milk or water.

TO COOK: for each serving mix 3 tbsp of porridge oats with 200 ml of milk or water in a microwave-safe jug or bowl, cook for $3\frac{1}{2}$ minutes and stir twice. When cooked stir well and leave to **stand** for 2 minutes. For 2 servings cook on high for 5 minutes.

portable oven Most microwave ovens are portable, in as much as they can be easily moved because they simply require a firm work surface, table or trolley to stand on near an electric socket. The larger the oven the higher the output has to be, therefore a smaller model may be more suitable for ovens that need to be moved regularly. Small portable ovens with a 500 W output are often installed in offices and are used for reheating food.

potato A starchy, white tuber with brown or red skin eaten as a **vegetable**. Potatoes are sometimes referred to as 'waxy types', which are moist, and these are best for salads and for frying because they stay firm. Those with a dry, fluffy texture are known as 'floury' and these potatoes are best for mashing, boiling and baking in their jackets. Potatoes can be 'baked' and boiled in the microwave, but they cannot be fried. Roasted potatoes can only be cooked in a **combination oven**.

There are many varieties of potato. New potatoes should be small, even-sized and thin-skinned, free from dirt and bruises. Mature potatoes should be firm, smooth and well-shaped, free from blemishes, cuts and sprouts and with very few 'eyes'. Avoid any damp or green potatoes. Always store them in a cool, dry, fairly dark place with good ventilation.

TO COOK: new potatoes: wash 450 g, prick their skins and put them into a dish with 2 tbsp of water. Cover the dish and cook on high for 8–10 minutes, stirring once. Drain, season and serve.

To cook boiled potatoes: peel 450 g, cut them into even-sized pieces and put them into a dish with 4 tbsp of water. Cover the dish and cook on high for 7–10 minutes, stirring once. Allow to **stand** for 3 minutes. Drain and serve or mash with 15 g of butter and a little milk and seasoning.

To cook jacket potatoes: wash and dry the potatoes, prick the skins and stand on absorbent paper on the floor of the oven. If cooking several, arrange them evenly spaced in a circle. Cook 1, 150 g potato on high for 5 minutes, 2 for 6–8 minutes, 3 for 9–10 minutes and 4 for 10–12 minutes. For potatoes weighing 350 g; cook on high 1 for 8 minutes, 2 for 15 minutes, 3 for 21 minutes and 4 for 27 minutes. Rearrange the potatoes halfway through the cooking time and allow them to stand for 3 minutes.

Chips cannot be fried in the microwave, but frozen oven chips can be cooked in a **browning dish**.

pottery Containers made of sturdy china or pottery are suitable for microwave cookery. Do not use pottery or earthenware if it is not covered with a glaze on the outside as well as inside, because it may absorb moisture and become hot. See also **cookware**.

poultry The meat of domestic fowls. All poultry can be cooked in the microwave provided it is young and tender. The flesh of the bird keeps moist and has a good taste and texture. Cook whole birds in a **roasting dish** and small ones in a **roasting bag** to promote browning. If the bird is stuffed, add time to the cooking. Turn the bird at least once during cooking. Cover wing tips with small pieces of **foil** to prevent them from drying out. **Standing time** is important because the temperature continues to rise at this stage and the cooking continues. See **chicken**; **duck**; **goose**; **poussin**; **turkey**.

poussin A young chicken (4–6 weeks old) usually weighing a maximum of 500 g (1lb) and sold whole.

TO COOK: cover the wings and leg tips and the breastbone with smooth pieces of **foil** to prevent over cooking. Put the bird into a pierced **roasting bag**, and place it breast-side down in a **roasting dish**. Cook on medium allowing 7–9 minutes per 450 g and turn over halfway. If using a thermometer, remove the poussin when it reads 82–85°C. Allow to **stand** for 15 minutes when the temperature will rise to 85–87°C. During standing time always **tent** a poussin with foil to keep it warm. To test if the bird is done, pierce the thickest part of the thigh with a skewer and the juices should run clear without a trace of pink.

power level See **variable power control**.

power output A term used to describe the wattage of a microwave oven.

prawn Any of various small, pink, mild-tasting **shellfish**. There are many varieties and sizes of raw and cooked prawns. Jumbo prawns, also called Mediterranean prawns, king prawns or crevettes, are the largest prawns available. Dublin Bay prawn, also known as scampi or langoustine are another popular large prawn. They are available in their shells or shelled, with or without their heads. Raw prawns cook successfully in the microwave, retaining their natural juices and flavour. When buying any variety of prawn what matters most is freshness, with poor handling or long storage they can deteriorate very quickly.

Prawns may be shelled and de-veined before of after cooking in the microwave (refer to the recipe used). To peel, break or cut off the head, remove the tail and shell. The tail can be left on depending on the recipe. De-vein by slitting down the centre of the back with a very finely bladed knife.

Medium-sized prawns are the most commonly eaten prawns and form the basis of a seafood menu. They are nearly always bought ready cooked. To heat cooked prawns in the microwave, put on a plate and cover. Add garlic butter if desired and cook 225 g for 2 minutes. Raw prawns are cooked in the same way until they turn pink. See also **shrimp**.

preserves Small amounts of preserves and relishes can be cooked successfully and quickly in the microwave. The ingredients do not stick and are unlikely to burn because there is no direct heat to the bowl. Make sure that the bowl is large and deep enough for the ingredients to bubble up without boiling over.

The fruits and vegetables should be finely chopped, then cooked with the sugar, vinegar and flavouring ingredients to a thick sauce with no excess liquid. Stir regularly in order to redistribute the sugar in the mixture so that it cooks evenly. Pour into hot sterilized jars, cover with acid-proof lids then store in a cool dark place. Pickles, **chutneys** and relishes need to mature for at least two months before eating.

prickly pear A yellow-orange or red-purple, sweet-tasting **fruit** of the cactus family covered with sharp bristles. Select undamaged fruit with a good colour. Wash them under running water and brush with a vegetable brush to remove the bristles (wear rubber gloves while preparing) and then slice off the skin. Prickly pears can be puréed and sieved for use in desserts or made into jam.

prune A dried plum, with a dark, wrinkled appearance. Most of the prunes available are quite moist and can be used uncooked, and they can be stuffed, chopped and added to stuffings, casseroles, cakes or puddings. See also **dried fruit**.

pulses The edible seeds of leguminous plants, such as beans, peas and lentils. Pulses are highly nutritious and are particularly important in the diets of vegetarians. Pulses will keep for many years, but they become drier and harder with time. Buy small quantities of bright, shiny pulses with no trace of dust, damp or mould.

TO PREPARE: pulses for cooking, put into a bowl and cover with water, discard any that float, drain and pick them over removing any stones and damaged seeds. While lentils and split peas do not need soaking, other larger pulses do.

Put the pulses into a deep bowl, cover with water and leave to soak 6–8 hours overnight. Drain and then rinse again. Alternatively, put 150–300 g of dried beans into a large bowl with 500 ml of water. Cover the bowl tightly and cook on high for 15 minutes. Allow to **stand** for 5 minutes and then uncover and add 500 ml of boiling water. Re-cover the bowl and leave to stand for 1 hour, then drain. See **adzuki bean; beans; black-eyed bean; black kidney bean; borlotti bean; broad bean; butter bean; cannellini bean; chickpea; flageolet; haricot bean; red kidney bean; lentil; mung bean; pea; soya bean**.

pumpkin   A large, round fruit with a tough, orange rind and pulpy orange flesh. Select clean, unblemished pumpkins that are heavy for their size. Whole pumpkin keeps longer than cut pumpkin. To use, cut the amount

required off the whole pumpkin, remove the
seeds and skin. Cut into chunky pieces before
cooking. It may be served as a vegetable or
added to casseroles. It may also be puréed and
used in soups, sauces or in a dessert pie.

TO COOK: place 450 g of pumpkin into a shallow dish and add 2 tbsp of water. Cover the dish
and cook on high for 5–6 minutes until tender.
Allow to **stand** for 2 minutes. See also **pumpkin
seed**.

pumpkin seed   The smooth, green, nutritious
seed of the **pumpkin**. Pumpkin seeds are usually
sold as a snack, but they may also be sprinkled
over food to add flavour and texture.

purée   A smooth, thick pulp of sieved, usually cooked, food.

quail A small **game** bird. Quail is available fresh all year round because most quail are farmed or frozen. They weigh on average about 150 g so allow 1 or 2 per person. The flesh is very delicate and care needs to be taken to prevent it from drying out, so wrap the bird in bacon or fat. Skewer the legs to the body with wooden cocktail sticks.

TO COOK: place 4 quail in a pierced **roasting bag**, then put them into a dish and cook on high for 6–8 minutes, rearranging once during cooking. Allow to **stand** for 2 minutes, during this time they may be lightly coloured under a grill.

quantity of food The length of cooking time is dependent on the amount of food in the oven. This is because the same amount of energy has to be absorbed by fewer or more items. If the amount of food in the microwave is doubled the cooking time should be increased by about half again.

quiche A savoury tart with a pastry case and a filling of eggs, milk and a selection of other ingredients, which may include meat, poultry, fish, vegetables and cheese. Cook the pastry case blind, fill with mixture and cook according to the recipe. A quiche may appear soft or wet in the centre but it will set completely when left to stand. Generally, microwave quiches do not look as appetizing as conventionally cooked ones.

174

TO REHEAT: put slices of quiche on a plate with the thin points towards the centre. Cook uncovered, allowing 1 minute for 1 slice, $1\frac{1}{2}$ for 2 and $2\frac{1}{2}$ for 4. If reheating bough quiche follow the instructions on the packet.

quick frying Stir-fried and sautéed dishes can be adapted successfully to the microwave. Use tender cuts of meat for best results. Quick frying uses only a small quantity of oil or butter and the food is stirred frequently.

quince A pear-shaped, brownish-yellow **fruit** with hard, sour flesh. Select plump, well-shaped, evenly coloured fruit with undamaged skins. Peel and core then cut into quarters. Quinces need to be cooked to improve their flavour, and can be used in pies, puddings or to make jam.

rabbit A small **game** mammal. Like other game, wild rabbit is lean and must be kept moist during cooking. The meat of domestic rabbit is light and delicate, very similar to chicken, and is tender enough to be used in sauté dishes. Rabbit is usually bought in joints.

TO COOK: cook with enough liquid to cover the meat and add carrots and onion. Cook 450 g of rabbit on high for 5 minutes and then on medium for 15 minutes. Add other flavourings and seasonings to taste and turn over and rearrange the portions during cooking. Allow to **stand** for 5 minutes.

raisin A dried black grape. The common 'seedless raisin' is widely available and used in cakes, biscuits, pudding or eaten as snacks or added to muesli and salads. Other varieties include the Lexia raisin and muscatel, which are much larger and juicer varieties and are excellent in Christmas pudding. See also **dried fruit**.

ramekin A small, ovenproof dish with deep sides, used for a single serving of food. Excellent for poached eggs, baked egg custard and cooking small cakes. See also **cookware**.

raspberry The red soft **fruit** of the raspberry plant, made up of many tiny, soft pods round a white core. Choose plump, brightly coloured fruit. Rinse carefully before use and dry on absorbent paper. Add to fruit salads or use in fruit tarts, sorbets, ice cream and desserts.

ravioli   A type of **pasta** in the form of small squares stuffed with a savoury or sweet filling.

rearranging food   Food items that cannot be stirred, such as baked potatoes and beef burgers, need to be moved around during cooking to ensure that they are evenly cooked. Turn the food at the same time and move items from the edge to the centre, from the back to the front, so that nothing remains in the same position while cooking.

redcurrant   A small, rounded, shiny red fruit, which grows in bunches and is related to the blackcurrant. Choose firm, fully ripe fruit and remove the stems before cooking. Redcurrants are very tart and need to be cooked with sugar if they are to be puréed and used in desserts.
   TO COOK: put 450 g of redcurrants into a dish with 2 tbsp of water and add 100 g of sugar. Cover the dish and cook on high for 3–4 minutes, stirring once. Add to mixed fruit pies or crumbles, or make sorbet, ice cream, cheesecake, soufflé or mousse.

red kidney bean   One of the most popular **pulses**, they are used in South American and

Mexican cookery. Red kidney beans are commonly used in the dish chilli con carne, and are also enjoyed in many vegetarian dishes.

TO COOK: soak the beans, then put them into a large dish and cover with fresh boiling water. Cover the dish and cook on high, ensuring that the beans are boiling hard for the first 10 minutes, and allow 20–30 minutes for 225 g of beans, stir 2 or 3 times during cooking. Leave to **stand** for 5–10 minutes. Cook for a further 5–10 minutes if still hard.

red lentil The orange-coloured lentil is a tiny **pulse** and is bought already skinned and split; it has a spicy flavour. Pick over the lentils before cooking and remove any small stones, then rinse in a sieve. Red lentils do not need to be soaked before cooking.

TO COOK: place 225 g of red lentils in a bowl and cover them with boiling water. Cover the bowl and cook on high for 10–12 minutes, stirring during cooking. Allow to **stand** for 5–10 minutes.

red mullet See **mullet**.

reflection A microwave oven cavity is made of metal, which reflects the microwaves without absorbing them. When the oven is operating the microwaves bounce off the metal surfaces of the walls, ceiling and floor in a regular pattern.

reheating Food can be reheated in the microwave with no loss of flavour, colour or texture, and the fast reheating times ensure minimal loss of vitamins. The techniques used for cooking foods in the microwave also apply when reheating them. Cover to prevent drying out, stir food occasionally for even heating and rearrange foods that cannot be stirred.

Foods in a sauce reheat better than those without, and so it is a good idea to cover slices or small pieces of meat or poultry with gravy. Soups reheat more quickly as individual portions, either in a mug or bowl. Stir them during heating. Small containers, such as mugs or jugs, do not need a lid, but larger casseroles need covering.

Dry foods, such as bread and pastry, should be reheated on absorbent kitchen paper to prevent the bottom of the food from becoming soggy. Use low power to reheat fish to prevent overcooking.

When reheating plates of food, make sure the food is evenly distributed on the plate, with thicker items towards the outside of the plate. Stacking rings can be used to heat more than one plate of food at the same time. Turn the plates a half turn during cooking. The food is reheated when the bottom of the plate feels warm (see also **plated meals**). See also APPENDIX III, REHEATING COOKED AND CONVENIENCE FOODS.

removable floor   A glass tray on the floor of some microwave ovens that do not have a turntable, which can be removed to be cleaned.

rhubarb   The sour, pink leafstalk of the rhubarb plant. Choose young fresh stems to avoid any stringiness. Wash the stems thoroughly, trim off the tops and bottoms then cut into pieces approximately 2–5 cm in length. Rhubarb is commonly used in pies, tarts and crumbles.

TO COOK: place 450 g of prepared rhubarb in a dish and add 3 tbsp of water. Cover the dish and cook on high for 7–8 minutes, stirring twice during cooking. Then stir in 100 g of sugar towards the end of the cooking time. Allow to **stand** for 3 minutes. Add cinnamon, orange or ginger to the rhubarb for an interesting flavour. Cooked rhubarb also makes a delicious fruit fool.

rice   The small, oval grains of a grass. Although there are many varieties of rice they can be divided into four main groups: longgrain, medium grain, short-grain and glutinous. Brown rice is also available, which is rice that has part or all of the outer husk remaining. Long-grain cooks into loose grains, of which there are two types: Basmati and Patna (or American long grain). These types of rice are suitable for pilafs, rice salads or any dish where a fluffy texture is preferred. The medium grain,

Carolina rice is often used for puddings and risottos. It breaks up more during cooking and clings together.

Short grain rice absorbs the most liquid and cooks to a creamy mass, which makes it suitable for puddings. Glutinous rice is shorter and rounder and is the rice eaten in Japan and other Far Eastern countries. It becomes quite sticky on cooking. Rice flakes, ground rice and rice flour are also available.

Very little time is saved by cooking rice in the microwave. However, it does not stick, boil over or need to be stirred when cooked in the microwave. In the microwave rice is cooked by the absorption method, which means that the rice absorbs all the liquid during cooking.

TO COOK: rinse 225 g of rice in cold water, put into a large bowl, pour over 600 ml of boiling water and add 1 tsp of salt. Cover the bowl and cook on high for 10 minutes. Allow to **stand** for 5 minutes then fluff up the grains with a fork. For brown rice add 750 ml of water to 225 g of rice and cook on high for 25–30 minutes, depending on the brand. See also **rice pudding**.

rice pudding   A milk pudding made with **rice**. Although rice can be used to make a wide range of desserts, the most popular is probably rice pudding. To prepare a simple rice pudding, cook the rice in milk flavoured with vanilla essence.

TO COOK: measure 50 g of pudding rice into a large bowl, and stir in 25 g of sugar and 600 ml of milk. Cover the bowl and cook on high for 8–10 minutes until it is boiling. Stir well and then cook on low for 30 minutes, stirring every 10 minutes. Allow to **stand** for 5 minutes.

To heat canned rice pudding, first empty the pudding into a microwave-proof dish. Cover the dish and cook on high for 2½ minutes, stirring twice during cooking.

ring mould A mould made from plastic, which is very useful when cooking foods that cannot be stirred. The central space of a ring mould ensures good heat distribution, because it allows the microwaves to reach the food through the inside as well as the outside. It is used for cakes, meat loaves, hot puddings and savarins.

roasting bag A bag large enough to contain joints of meat or whole poultry and a microwave roasting dish. The roasting bag is designed to prevent splattering and to help promote browning. Use a bag large enough to contain both the joint and microwave roasting dish, so the meat or chicken is raised out of the cooking juices. Use string or an elastic band to secure the bag, not metal twist ties which could cause **arcing**. Pierce bags before cooking to allow steam to escape. If the bag is too small, slash it along one side and make a tent over the joint of meat.

roasting dish A dish made from a ceramic or rigid plastic material, usually available with a rack. A roasting dish is designed for cooking meats and poultry because the rack allows the juices to drip out while cooking. Roasting dishes can also be used for reheating bread and rolls, and cooking anything that benefits from the all-round action of microwave energy, such as cakes and meat loaves.

roe The milt of the male fish (soft roe) usually herring or flounder, or the eggs of the female fish (hard roe) and usually comes from cod.

TO COOK: soft roes, wash carefully and dry on absorbent paper. Put 15 g of butter into a dish, melt on high for 30 seconds. Add 225 g of roes and coat with butter, cover and cook on high for 2 minutes. **Stand** for 1 minute, season and then serve on hot toast.

rose coco bean See **borlotti bean**.

rosemary The aromatic grey-green leaves of a European shrub used as a **herb**. Traditionally used in lamb dishes, it is also used with vegetables, pasta, paté and breadmaking.

rotating antenna A slatted metal disc concealed below the oven floor or above the ceiling of the oven, which rotates by the action of the air from the cooking system. Microwave ovens that do not have a turntable may incorporate a rotating antenna to aid in the more even distribution of microwaves.

rotating dish To ensure even cooking, foods that cannot be stirred, such as lasagne and cakes, need to be given a half or quarter turn at intervals throughout the cooking time. Make sure to rotate the dish in one direction only. This is usually unnecessary if your oven has a turntable.

runner bean (also called **string bean**) The fibrous, immature pod of the scarlet runner bean plant. Choose young, firm, fresh-coloured beans free from blemishes. Wash the beans, remove tops and tails and remove any strings. Cut into short lengths or slice thinly using a special bean slicer if available.

TO COOK: put 225 g of prepared beans into a dish and add 2 tbsp of water. Cover the dish and cook on high for 6 minutes, stirring 2–3 times during cooking. Allow to **stand** for 2 minutes.

safety of a microwave oven   All microwave ovens are designed with a safety mechanism that ensures the oven cannot operate unless the door is shut and the start button pushed. Use the microwave oven only to defrost, heat and cook food, and use microwave-safe cookware and utensils. Do not turn the microwave on when the oven is empty. The microwave is safe to use as the sides both inside the oven and outside do not become hot, there are no naked flames and items are stable inside the oven during cooking. Remember to use oven gloves to remove dishes from the microwave and carefully peel back film or remove lids towards you to avoid escaping steam, which can cause scalding.

saffron   The dried yellow-orange stigmas of crocus flowers used to flavour and colour food especially sauces and rice dishes.

sage   The grey-green leaves of a perennial Mediterranean plant used as a **herb**. Sage is traditionally used with onion to make stuffing, but it also goes well with cheese and egg dishes.

sago   A starchy cereal obtained from the pith of the trunk of the sago palm. Sago is available in granules and is traditionally used to make puddings and sweet dishes, and can be added to soups to thicken.

TO COOK: to make sago pudding put 50 g of sago into a large bowl, stir in 25 g of sugar and 600 ml of milk. Cover the bowl and cook on high for 8–10 minutes until boiling. Stir well and then continue to cook on low for 30 minutes, stirring every 10 minutes, until thick and creamy. Allow to **stand** for 5 minutes.

saithe (also called **coalfish** or **coley**) A white fish with a bland flavour, which is best used in fish pies or soups.

TO COOK: place saithe fillet into a dish with the thickest parts towards the outside. Cover the dish and cook 225 g on high for 2½–3 minutes and 450 g for 3–4 minutes. Allow to **stand** for 2 minutes.

salmon A soft-finned, fatty fish native to the Atlantic and Pacific Oceans. A mature salmon is a large, strong fish varying in skin colour. Its flesh is firm with a medium to large flake, pink in colour and rich in flavour. Wild salmon and salmon trout are seasonal fish, but farmed salmon is available throughout the year. A large capacity oven without a turntable is required to cook a small whole salmon, otherwise the salmon must be curved into a dish. Alternatively, the salmon can be cut into two pieces, which may be placed in to a **roasting bag** or on a large plate and then reassembled on the serving dish. The joins can be covered by decoration. Cold salmon looks particularly effective when covered with wafer-thin slices of peeled cucumber.

Salmon steaks, usually up to an inch thick, are always available as are fillets and cutlets.

TO COOK: for a whole salmon, cut up if necessary on to a large plate or dish, if too long remove the head. **Shield** the tail with foil and season the cavity with salt, pepper, lemon juice and sprigs of dill or parsley. Sprinkle 4 tbsp of dry white wine over the fish. Cover with **clingfilm** or wrap in **greaseproof paper**. Cook the salmon on high for 4 minutes per 450 g, turning it once during the cooking time. Allow to **stand** covered for 5 minutes if serving hot, or leave until cold then skin, fillet and garnish.

To cook salmon steaks, place them in a dish, with the narrow ends towards the centre, and brush with oil or melted butter. Cover the dish and cook on high, allowing 3 minutes per 225 g of fish and turning once during cooking. Allow to stand for 1 minute. A **browning dish** can be used if preferred.

salmonella A bacteria that causes **food poisoning**. Raw, untreated milk, eggs, meat and poultry can be contaminated on the farm. Salmonella breeds in food at room temperature, but it cannot reproduce under refrigeration. It is destroyed by temperatures above 60°C, therefore it is important to always make sure food is properly and thoroughly cooked to avoid any risks. Salmonella poisoning should always be diagnosed and treated by a doctor.

salsify A root **vegetable** with a delicate, oyster-like flavour. Choose roots that are as smooth and firm as possible. Peel, trim and put the salsify into acidulated water (water with lemon juice added to it) to prevent discoloration, then cut into pieces about 5–8 cm long.

TO COOK: put the prepared salsify into a dish with 2 tbsp of water. Cook 225 g on high for 6–7 minutes, stirring once during cooking. Allow to **stand** for 3 minutes.

sardine A small, immature, fatty **fish** of the herring family (usually a pilchard). Sardines are eaten fresh or canned in oil or tomato sauce.

TO COOK: remove the gut, wash the fish carefully and score the skin down both sides. Heat a **browning dish** for 5 minutes and then add 2 tbsp of olive oil and the sardines. Cover the dish with **greaseproof paper** and cook on high for 4–5 minutes per 450 g of fish, turn them over after a third of the cooking time. **Stand** for 3 minutes and serve with herbs or garlic butter and lemon.

satsuma A small **citrus fruit** with bright orange rind and sweet juicy orange flesh, eaten fresh or used in desserts, sauces and marmalade.

sauce A sauce may have a variety of functions: it can moisten and enhance the flavour of food; or as a bland flavour, such as white sauce, provide a contrast to stronger flavoured food. Sauces can be made quickly in the microwave, without the risk of sticking or becoming lumpy. Always use a container large enough to prevent sauces boiling over. Most sauces are cooked on high power, but delicate egg-based sauces, such as Hollandaise, Bearnaise and **custard**, are best cooked on medium. The lower temperature prevents boiling, which would result in curdling. Dessert sauces are quick and easy to make in the microwave as toppings for ice cream and desserts. See also **bread sauce**; **gravy**.

sausage Finely minced or ground meat, especially pork or beef, mixed with fat, cereal or bread seasonings then cased in a skin. Sausages may also contain added offal, gristle and connective tissue. They cook quickly in the microwave, but the finished result does not look very appetizing. A **browning dish** can be used to improve their colour and they can be brushed over with a **browning agent**, which also enhances their colour. Prick the sausages before cooking or the skins will burst.

TO COOK: first pre-heat a browning dish if being used. Cook 225 g of sausages on high for 4–5 minutes and 450 g for 6–7 minutes, turning them over and rearranging several times during cooking. See also **bockwurst**; **bratwurst**; **chipolata**; **frankfurter**.

scallop Any of various bivalve molluscs. Scallops are available in shell and ready shelled. The tiny scallops are called 'queen scallops', which are a different species and not just under-sized scallops.

Remove the brown vein from the cleaned scallops. The orange roe needs to be separated from the white meat because it does not take as long to cook and bursts if overcooked. Halve or slice the white meat depending on the size of the scallop.

TO COOK: place the white meat in a dish with 2 tbsp of dry white wine and season to taste. Cover the dish and cook 225 g on high for $1\frac{1}{2}$ minutes, stir scallops and add the coral. Cook for a further minute. Add 3–4 tbsp of cream blended with 1 tsp of cornflour and heat through for a further minute, until thickened. Allow to **stand** for 2 minutes.

scampi (also called **Dublin Bay prawn** or **langoustine**) Large **prawns** although they are in fact a small member of the lobster family.

Scampi have a fragile texture and taste and are sold both cooked and raw, with or without heads.

scone A small doughy cake. Scones are made with a simple dough, based on flour and milk, and raised with baking powder. They rise well and quickly in the microwave, but always follow a recipe designed specifically for cooking in a microwave. Scones can be sweet or savoury depending on the ingredients added to the dough. They can also be made either entirely with wholemeal flour or a just a proportion, which helps to improve their otherwise pale colour. A batch of eight scones takes about 4 minutes to cook on full power.

seasoning Salt, pepper, **herbs** and **spices** are essential ingredients in cooking, because they develop and improve the flavour of other ingredients. Some other seasoning ingredients, such as saffron, wine and vanilla essence, also add their own distinctive flavour. It is important that any seasoning added should not be over-used otherwise the dish could easily be spoilt. It is difficult to assess how much seasoning is needed in a recipe because individual taste and the nature of the ingredients can vary. It is better to under-season during cooking, then taste the food at the end and adjust if necessary.

sea trout A silvery, marine variety of brown **trout**, sometimes called salmon trout because of its similarity in appearance and colour (but it is not as expensive).

TO COOK: for a whole sea trout, cut up if necessary on to a large plate or dish and if too long remove the head. **Shield** the tail with foil and season the cavity with salt, pepper, lemon juice and sprigs of dill or parsley. Sprinkle 4 tbsp of dry white wine over the fish. Cover with microwave-safe **clingfilm** or wrap in **grease-proof paper**. Cook the trout on high for 4 minutes per 450 g, turning it once during the cooking time. Allow to **stand** covered for 5 minutes if serving hot or leave until cold then skin, fillet and garnish.

To cook trout steaks, place them in a dish, with the narrow ends towards the centre, and brush with oil or melted butter. Cover the dish and cook on high, allowing 3 minutes per 225 g of fish, turning once during cooking. Allow to stand for 1 minute. A **browning dish** can be used if preferred.

seeds The hard fruits of plants. There are many seeds that are eaten as foods, such as **sesame seeds** and **caraway seeds**. Some are used to flavour bread, biscuits and cakes and some, such as sunflower and **pumpkin seeds**, are added to muesli or eaten alone as snacks. See also **poppy seeds**.

semolina A grainy powder made from hard or durum wheat. Semolina is granular in appearance and its colour may range from a clear yellow (durum) to a pale beige (hard wheat). Durum semolina is used for making pasta products, such as spaghetti. Hard wheat semolina is used to make puddings and cakes, couscous and breakfast cereals.

TO COOK: to make semolina pudding put 50 g of semolina into a large bowl, stir in 25 g of sugar and 600 ml of milk. Cover the bowl and cook on high for 8–10 minutes until boiling. Stir well and then continue to cook on low for 30 minutes, stirring every 10 minutes, until thick and creamy. Allow to **stand** for 5 minutes.

sesame seed The tiny, golden, oily seed of a tropical herbaceous plant of East Indian origin. Sesame seeds have a nutty aroma, which is accentuated when they are baked or roasted. They are added to salads, vegetable dishes, casseroles, meat loaves, quiches and stuffings. They can be used to coat food, sprinkled on scones, loaves and bread rolls or made into a paste.

TO TOAST: put 75 g of sesame seeds into a shallow dish and heat them on high for 3–5 minutes until golden, stirring twice during heating.

shallot A small bulb related to the **onion**, with a sweet, intense taste. Shallots are used in cooking to add flavour, but they should not be allowed to overcook and brown as this causes them to become bitter.

shape and size of food It is important that food cooked in the microwave should be as uniform in shape and size as possible, so that it is cooked evenly and at the same rate. The thinner parts of food cook faster than the thicker areas and small pieces of food cook faster than large ones. See also **arranging food**.

shelf A removable metal shelf, available on some microwaves, that increases the amount of food that can be cooked in the oven or can be used in conjunction with the **browning grill**. It may be possible to have the shelf in two different positions or it may be removed from the oven when not required. It is useful for cooking or reheating several items of food at the same time. Complete meals can be cooked in a one or two step operation, but it does require careful planning. Those that require the longest cooking time are placed on the shelf while those that require shorter cooking time or heating times are placed on the **glass tray**. This is because the microwave starts cooking the foods at the top of the oven first. Remember, as the amount of food being cooked is increased, cooking time must also be increased. In most cases, the cooking of a complete meal at one time does not save a significant amount of cooking time compared to conventional cooking.

shellfish A general term for edible crustaceans and molluscs. Shellfish should always be bought fresh and cooked (except **oysters**, which are often eaten raw). Shellfish can be cooked in the microwave, but they need very careful timing. Overcooking toughens the flesh and makes the shellfish inedible. See **clam**; **crab**; **crayfish**; **lobster**; **mussel**: **prawn**; **scallop**; **shrimp**.

shielding The term used to describe the process of protecting vulnerable parts of food in order to prevent them from overcooking. The thin ends of meat, bone tips, meat near the bone and the cut edges of meat joints and poultry should be shielded with smooth strips of aluminium **foil**. Tails and heads of large fish should be covered for the first half of cooking time. The amount of food left uncovered must be much greater than the area shielded by foil. Shielding can also be useful when using a square or rectangular container, to prevent the corners from overcooking. The dish must then be covered with greaseproof paper or microwave-safe clingfilm to prevent **arcing**.

shortbread A rich, crumbly biscuit made with a high proportion of fat. Shortbread is very difficult to prepare successfully in the microwave. It tends to be pale and the centre may burn. It is best prepared in a conventional oven.

shrimp Any of various tiny, crustacean **shell-fish**, which are usually sold cooked. Shrimps can be incorporated into many seafood dishes, soups, fish terrines or made into potted shrimps.

skate A large, fatty fish of the ray family. The wings of skate are the only part eaten. Choose small tender wings weighing about 225 g each.

TO COOK: cook 450 g of skate wings dotted with butter. Arrange on a dish with the thinner ends towards the centre and **shield** the tips with foil. A pre-heated **browning dish** can be used. Cover the dish and cook on high for 4 minutes, turning over halfway. Allow to **stand** for 3 minutes and serve with melted butter and chopped capers.

skewer A long pin, which may be used to test if a cake is done, after standing time. The skewer should come out cleanly when inserted. Do not use metal skewers to secure meat or poultry; tie with string and use cocktail sticks in place of small metal skewers to secure the neck flap of poultry.

smoked food Foods, usually meat, poultry, game, fish and cheese, that have been preserved by hanging them in smoke, traditionally that from a wood fire. The food is preserved by drying and by the action of a range of chemicals contained in the smoke.

snail A mollusc with a spirally coiled shell. Snails have chewy flesh with a delicate flavour and just a hint of earthiness. They are available in can and are packed separately from their shells. Canned snails are pre-cooked and require only to be placed into their shells and reheated.

TO COOK: place the snails in a dish and dot with garlic butter. Cover the dish and cook on high for $1\frac{1}{2}$–2 minutes.

sole A general name for several species of flat, white **fish** including Dover sole and lemon sole. Sole is considered to be the best of all flatfish with its firm flesh and delicate flavour. It can be cooked whole or in fillets, which can be stuffed and rolled. The dark skin should always be removed before cooking.

TO COOK: place a whole sole weighing approximately 350 g in a dish and dot with butter. Cover the dish and cook on high for 3–4 minutes. Allow to **stand** for 1 minute and then serve with the cooking juices. For 450 g of fillets, cook on high for 2–3 minutes.

sorrel A leafy vegetable that is similar to spinach. Sorrel has a bitter, slightly sour taste and the young leaves have a hint of lemon. It is often cooked like spinach, but eaten in small quantities. A few leaves can add interest to soups, or chopped and added to sauces, omelettes and salads.

TO COOK: put into a large bowl, cover and cook 225 g on high for 2–3 minutes and 450 g for 3–4 minutes, stirring halfway through. Drain and season.

soufflé A very light dish made with egg yolks and stiffly beaten egg whites combined with various ingredients, such as fish or cheese. Soufflés can be cooked in the microwave, but they are not as successful as those prepared in a conventional oven. They rise and fall several times during cooking in the microwave and fall quickly when removed from the oven, and they do not form a crust.

soup A liquid food made from a variety of ingredients that are boiled or simmered. Consommés (clear soups), bisques (shellfish soup), vegetable purées, creams and broths are all types of soup. Almost any ingredient can be used in a soup, including meat, fish, poultry vegetables, cereals and dairy products. Most soups can be made successfully in the microwave, as well as the stock which is an essential base of most good soups. Add hot stock or liquid to the ingredients to save cooking time.

The microwave is also useful for heating canned soups (remove from the can first), cooking frozen soup and making dried packet soup. Soups should be stirred during cooking to equalize the temperature.

To reheat canned or home-made soup place 300 ml in 2 bowls. Cook on high for 4 minutes, stirring once.

soya bean A small, oval **pulse** or legume, commonly cream-yellow in colour. The bean takes a long time to cook and has a floury texture. It is used in soups, stews, casseroles and salads. Many products, such as miso, soy sauce, tempeh, soya milk and tofu, are made from soya beans.

TO COOK: after soaking, rinse the beans and place them in a large dish, and immerse with fresh boiling water. Cover the dish and cook 225 g of beans on high for 20–30 minutes, ensuring that the beans are boiling hard for the first 10 minutes, and stir 2 or 3 times during cooking. Leave to **stand** for 5–10 minutes and cook for a further 5–10 minutes if still hard.

soya oil The oil obtained from the **soya bean**. It is pale yellow with a bland taste and is used for cooking.

soy sauce A spicy, dark sauce made from fermented soya beans and wheat, traditionally used in Chinese and far Eastern cooking. Varied processing techniques produce soya sauces with different flavours. Some sauces are very dark and strong, others are light and only mildly salty. Soy sauce can be used in marinades and as a **browning agent** brushed onto pale meats to improve their colour.

spaghetti A type of **pasta** in the form of long strings. Spaghetti is excellent with a sauce and is the most popular of all pastas.

TO COOK: place 225 g of white spaghetti in boiling water and cook on high for 7–8 minutes. For 225 g of wholemeal spaghetti also cook on high, but for 8–10 minutes.

spaghetti squash (also called **vegetable squash**) A large oval, deep yellow squash, which has a fibrous flesh that looks like spaghetti.

TO COOK: 1 squash approximately 1.2 kg. Cut in half, lengthways, place the halves cut-side down into a dish and add 3–4 tbsp of water. Cover the dish and cook on high for 9–10 minutes, or until tender, rotating the halves halfway through cooking. Allow to **stand** 3–4 minutes. Remove the spaghetti-like flesh with a fork. Toss in butter or olive oil and season well before serving.

sparking See **arcing**.

spices Any of a variety of seeds, stems or roots of aromatic plants that are used whole or ground to add flavour to food. Buy in small quantities and store in airtight jars. Many spices are best if they are bought whole, but ready-ground spices are usually more convenient to use. Spices are used to flavour both sweet and savoury dishes and some can be added in large quantities to thicken sauces. There are various spice mixtures available ready-prepared or they can be made up as required, these include curry powder, five-spice powder, garam masala, harissa, mixed spice and pickling spice.

spinach A leafy green vegetable, which can be used raw in salads or cooked. Choose fresh, green crisp leaves, wash and rinse well discarding any damaged leaves and pull away the midrib of larger leaves.

TO COOK: either (a), put into a large bowl, cover and cook 225 g on high for 2–3 minutes and 450 g for 3–4 minutes, stirring halfway through cooking; or (b), chop up the spinach and place it into a **roasting bag** without water and cook as above, shaking the bag during cooking. Drain and serve.

splash guard A feature of some microwave ovens that is designed to protect the wave stirrer from food splatterings. It should be cleaned regularly.

split pea A dried pea that has been skinned, which can be either green or yellow. Split peas cook quickly and do not need soaking before cooking. They make a good purée to serve as a vegetable accompaniment and are used in soup.

TO COOK: put the split peas into a large bowl and cover with boiling water. Cover the bowl and cook 225 g of peas for 15–20 minutes, then allow to **stand** for 5–10 minutes. See also **pulses**.

spring greens A variety of young cabbage, which are sold before the hearts have developed. Choose crisp and fresh spring greens. Remove all thick tough stalks, wash the leaves thoroughly and then shred.

TO COOK: put 450 g of prepared spring greens into a large bowl with 3 tbsp of water. Cover the bowl and cook on high for 6–7 minutes. Drain and season.

squash The large **fruit** of a marrow-like plant with a hard rind and a pulpy flesh. There are many varieties of squash, including **acorn squash**, **butternut squash**, hokido pumpkin, golden nugget, onion squash or **spaghetti squash**. They are all excellent included in casseroles and made into soups.

TO COOK: place 450 g of squash into a shallow dish and add 2 tbsp of water. Cover the dish and cook on high for 5–6 minutes until tender. Allow to **stand** for 2 minutes.

squid A torpedo-shaped, smooth, white-fleshed mollusc. Squid are available cleaned and prepared. Choose smaller ones with firm flesh. It may be cooked whole or cut into rings. It requires very little cooking and if overcooked quickly goes tough.

TO COOK: stuff a cleaned, whole squid, close its ends with cocktail sticks and place it into a dish with a savoury sauce. Cover the dish and cook 225 g of squid on high for 4–5 minutes. Allow to **stand** for 3 minutes.

To cook squid rings; place the rings into a large bowl with 150 ml of water or stock per 450 g of squid. Cover the bowl and cook on high for 5–8 minutes.

stacking ring A plastic ring that is used for stacking plates. An essential device for **reheating** more than one **plated meal** at a time. In an average-sized oven up to 3 plates can be stacked on these plastic rings. Remember to cover the top plate and also, because it receives more microwave energy than those below, change the order of the plates halfway through to ensure even cooking. When the underside of each plate feels hot all over the food is ready to serve.

stand See **standing time**.

standing time (also called **heat equalizing**) Sometimes referred to as heat equalizing, standing time is an essential part of the cooking process. The food is left to stand after it has been removed from the oven to finish cooking. The heat is passed from the outside to the centre of the food by conduction. The standing time will vary according to the size and density of the food. Because joints of meat may need to stand for a long time, they should be loosely wrapped in aluminium **foil** during the standing time to keep in the heat.

Recipes will state when standing times are necessary. If further cooking is needed after standing time there is no need to repeat the specified standing time.

steak A cut of lean meat (**beef, lamb** or **pork**) usually from the rump or loin of an animal. Steak is a good cut to use in microwave recipes because it will be lean and tender, and can be cooked quickly. For the best results use a preheated **browning dish**.

steaming A method of cooking by suspending the food over boiling water. Fish, chicken, vegetables and fruits are all suitable for steaming in the microwave. The small amount of liquid used is converted to steam when the dish is covered and the food cooks in the moisture.

stirrer fan (also called **wave stirrer**) A device designed to distribute the emerging microwaves evenly throughout the metal cooking cavity.

stirring As the outer edges of food normally cook first in the microwave, stir from the outside of the dish towards the centre to produce an evenly cooked result. To prevent food at the edges overcooking, dishes should be stirred at frequent intervals.

stock The juice obtained by boiling meat, poultry, fish or vegetables, or by adding water to stock cubes. A good stock is the basis of home-made soups and is used to make gravies and sauces. See also **chicken stock; fish stock**.

strawberry The sweet, fleshy red fruit of the strawberry plant. Strawberries are most often eaten with sugar and cream, but they are also excellent in fruit salad, used as a topping for cheesecake and to make jam, ice cream, fools or mousses.

string bean See **runner bean**.

suet A tough, dry, waxy deposit of fat found around certain organs of animals. Suet is most often bought prepared in shredded form and used to make suet pastry and steamed puddings. A healthier vegetable suet is also available.

sugar (also called **sucrose**) A substance that occurs naturally in beet and cane sugar, from which it is commercially refined. Sugar is available in many forms depending on its stage of refinement: white sugar (e.g. caster, granulated and icing sugar) and brown sugar (e.g. demerara and muscovado). It is used in preserves, confectionery, cakes, biscuits and desserts.

TO SOFTEN: brown sugar, place in a dish, add 1 apple wedge or a slice of white bread. Heat on high for 30–40 seconds. Allow to **stand** for 30 seconds. Remove the apple or bread and stir the sugar once.

To caramelize sugar, place 200 g of sugar in a 1 litre microwave-safe glass jug and add 3 tbsp of water. Cook on high for 5–7 minutes until the sugar is golden, without stirring.

sugar pea See **mangetout**.

sultana A dried white grape. Some sultanas are treated with sulphur dioxide, others are not, check the ingredients list on the packet. They are used in baking for cakes, Christmas pudding, mince pies as well as in muesli, salads and puddings. See also **dried fruit**.

sunflower oil The vegetable oil extracted from sunflower seeds. The refined oil is a pale yellow colour with a bland flavour. It is used for cooking and salad dressings, and in the manufacture of margarine.

sunflower seeds The small, highly nutritious seeds of the sunflower, with tough black- and white-striped skin and a smooth, oily stone-coloured kernel. Sunflower seeds are best stored in a glass, airtight jar in the refrigerator. Use raw in savoury vegetarian dishes, such as soups, stir-fries, rice and pasta. Roasted sunflower seeds can be added to salads or eaten as a snack. See also **seeds**.

swede A bulbous root **vegetable** with pulpy orange flesh and a pale yellow skin. Choose firm, clean swedes, which are heavy for their size. Swede is commonly cooked and served as a vegetable, but it is also used in soups, stews, casseroles, fritters and savoury vegetarian dishes.

TO COOK: peel the swede thickly, cut into chunky pieces and put into a dish with 2 tbsp of water. Cook 450 g on high for 8–9 minutes, stirring once or twice. Allow to **stand** for 2 minutes, drain, season and serve or mash with butter.

sweetbreads The pancreas or thymus gland of an animal, usually calf or lamb. Sweetbreads have a delicate flavour and creamy texture and are cooked in several stages. First they are soaked for a few hours and then blanched before cooking, and this is best done conventionally. After which as much of the membrane as possible needs to be removed.

TO COOK: thickly slice 450 g of sweetbreads and put into a dish with 150 ml of stock and a little butter. Cover the dish and cook on high for 8–10 minutes until tender. Allow to **stand** for 10 minutes. Use the liquid to make a sauce with cream.

sweetcorn The tender, sweet-tasting, yellow kernels of unripe maize. Sweetcorn is available frozen or in cans. If the kernels are still attached to the ear it is known as corn on the cob. The best sweetcorn should have the fresh green husk still attached and the silky threads between the husk and corn should feel damp. Avoid dry, yellow husks, small shrinking kernels and excessively large kernels. Remove the husks and silky threads before cooking.

TO COOK: place in a dish with 1 tbsp of water per cob. Cover the dish and cook on high, 1 cob for 4–5 minutes, 2 cobs 6–7 minutes, and 4 cobs 8–9 minutes, turn over halfway through cooking time. **Stand** for 3 minutes, drain, season and serve with butter.

To cook baby corn on the cob, which are available with husks removed, put 225 g into a dish, add 2 tbsp of water and cook on high for 3–4 minutes, turning halfway. Stand for 2 minutes, drain and serve.

To cook frozen sweetcorn kernels, put 225 g of kernels into a bowl, cover and cook on high for 4–5 minutes.

sweet making   See **confectionery**.

sweet pepper   See **peppers**.

sweet potato   The large, edible root of a tropical vine, eaten as a vegetable. Choose firm, undamaged sweet potatoes with either a pink skin, which has orange flesh, or a brown skin, which has yellow flesh. Brush clean, then peel thickly and cut into chunky pieces. Cook as for potato, they can also be cooked whole like a jacket potato.

swordfish   An extremely solid, firm-fleshed game **fish**, which is popular in Mediterranean countries and America, and is becoming increasingly available in the rest of Europe.

TO COOK: brush steaks with oil and wrap individually in greaseproof paper. Place onto a plate and cook on high; 1, 225 g steak for 3 minutes and 2 for 4–5 minutes. Allow to **stand** for 3 minutes.

syrup   A concentrated solution of sugar. Maple syrup is a natural extract of the maple tree and often served with pancakes. Other syrups, which include golden syrup and treacle, are the by-products obtained during the refining of sugar crystals. Syrups are useful for quickly glazing microwave puddings.

Tabasco sauce A thin, red, pungent sauce made from chillies, vinegar and salt. It may be used to enhance microwave meat dishes and casseroles and is used widely in Creole cuisine.

taco A folded tortilla (pancake), which is made from cornmeal then fried into a curved shape to make a taco shell. Tacos can be filled with a variety of savoury Mexican ingredients, such as chilli con carne.

TO HEAT: pre-cooked taco shells, place 8 on a piece of kitchen paper and heat on high for 1–2 minutes until warm. Spoon in the filling of your choice.

tagliatelle A type of **pasta** in the form of long, flat, ribbons, which may be plain, tomato or spinach flavoured.

TO COOK: place 225 g of tagliatelle in a dish, cover with boiling water and cook on high for 7 minutes.

tapioca A grainy starch obtained from the root of the cassava plant. Tapioca is available as pellets, flakes, granules or flour and is used in puddings and as a thickening agent.

TO COOK: to make tapioca pudding, put 3 tbsp of quick-cooking tapioca into a bowl with 600 ml of milk, 1 beaten egg and 3 tbsp of caster sugar. Cook on high for 10 minutes.

taro (also called **dasheen**) A large tuber vegetable with a dry texture and a taste similar to sweet potato. Its skin is light brown and rough in appearance. Taros are often available from West Indian shops and can be eaten as an alternative to potato.

TO COOK: peel and cut into 2.5 cm cubes. Put 450 g of taro into a dish with 4 tbsp of water. Cover the dish and cook on high for 8–10 minutes. Drain off the starchy cooking liquid before serving.

tarragon The small, toothed leaves of an aromatic, perennial plant that are used fresh or dried as a **herb**. Tarragon is an essential ingredient for Bearnaise and tartare sauces, and it may also be used with poultry, seafood, veal and egg dishes.

TO DRY: place a small bunch of leaves on a kitchen paper and cook on high for 25 seconds.

tea An infusion of dried, fermented leaves of one of several varieties of evergreen tropical or sub-tropical shrub. Tea can play a part in flavouring food, for example in sorbets, tea loaves and fruit bread, such as barm brack.

TO HEAT: pour the tea into a microwave-safe mug and heat on high for 1 minute.

temperature of food The starting temperature of food will affect microwave cooking. The colder the food the longer it will take to heat up or cook. For best results, defrost foods first, then cook them. Room temperatures also differ during the year so adjust cooking times accordingly. Cooking times given in recipes usually assume foods are taken from the place they are normally stored immediately before cooking, for example, meat and chicken will be chilled from the refrigerator.

temperature probe Some ovens have a temperature probe that fits into a socket inside the oven cavity. The probe is usually used for cooking joints of meat, but can be used with other foods. The probe is inserted into the thickest part of the food and is left in during cooking. The degree of cooking is selected and when the internal temperature reaches the pre-set level, the cooker switches itself off.

tenting A term used to describe the method of loosely covering meats and poultry with **foil** (with the shiny side towards the food) after cooking to retain heat during **standing time**.

thawing See **defrosting**.

thermometer An instrument used to measure temperature. Specially designed microwave-safe thermometers are made without mercury, so they can be used without being affected by microwave energy. Inserted into the meat about halfway through cooking time the internal temperature indicates the degree of cooking. The temperature will rise during **standing time** and each type of meat needs to reach a certain level.

Alternatively, a standard meat thermometer can be used to test the food outside the microwave. It should be inserted into the food immediately after it has been taken out of the microwave.

thyme The leaves of a temperate shrub with a strong mint-like odour and used as a **herb**. Thyme is one of the ingredients of a classic bouquet garni. It is used in savoury dishes, such as casseroles and stews.

TO DRY: place a small bunch onto kitchen paper and cook on high for 25 seconds.

timing Most recipes indicate the level of power (wattage) they have been tested at, usually this will be 650 W. If you are using a 500 W model add 25 seconds per minute, for 700 W deduct 15 seconds per minute. It is always better to undercook slightly, leave to stand then check if the food is cooked, rather than risk overcooking. See also **quantity of food**.

timing control A dial, pad or push button on the oven's control panel that is used to set the amount of cooking time required. Microwave cooking is based on time rather than temperature so it is best to choose models with clear and easy to use timing controls. Electronic touch controls are more accurate than the mechanical dial type. The timer will turn off the microwave energy automatically at the end of the cooking period.

tofu A smooth, bland curd made from the yellow soya bean and available either in a firm or silken junket-like form. Tofu is used extensively in vegetarian cooking, where it is cut into cubes or sliced and added to stir-fries, omelettes, soups, salads and other vegetable mixtures.

tomato The fleshy, red, many-seeded fruit of the tomato plant available all year. Choose well shaped, firm, red tomatoes, which are heavy for their size and with undamaged skins. There are several varieties categorized according to their shape and size. They are used in a variety of ways, including in salads, soups, sauces, casseroles, chutney or even stuffed.

To make it easier to peel tomatoes, put two into a bowl of boiling water and microwave them on high for 30 seconds until their skins split. Then put them into cold water and remove the skins.

tomato purée A thick red paste made from tomatoes with a strong flavour and smell.

215

Tomato purée is available in jars, cans or tubes and may be used in sauces, stews or soups. Once opened store the purée in the refrigerator.

tongue A type of **offal**, usually from an ox, lamb, calf or pig. Tongue needs long, slow cooking in plenty of liquid to soften it. First soak the tongue in salted water for 1 hour and then rinse, and trim away any bones and gristle.

TO COOK: place in a large bowl, cover with boiling water and add some peppercorns, onion, carrot and celery. Cover the bowl and cook a 1 kg tongue on high until boiling and then on medium for 65–70 minutes. Allow to **stand** for 10 minutes. Test it with a skewer for tenderness. Leave it in the water until it has cooled completely, then remove any fat and split the skin and peel it off.

Serve at once with parsley sauce or curl it into a dish, press and allow it to chill for 24 hours, and use it sliced in sandwiches and salads.

treacle A syrup obtained as a by-product from the refining of crystallized sugar. Treacle is thick and dark brown to black because it has been subject to very high temperatures and is very concentrated. Treacle is used in confectionery, Christmas puddings and rich fruit cakes. It is especially useful for puddings and cakes prepared in the microwave because it improves their colour.

tripe The stomach lining of sheep or ox, which is eaten as offal. Tripe is sold par-boiled and should be clean and white. Before cooking first soak it in cold water for 5–10 minutes, then rinse it thoroughly and cut into strips or small squares.

TO COOK: put 450 g of soaked tripe into a bowl, cover with milk or stock and add onion and herbs. Cook it on high until boiling and then continue to cook it on the defrost setting (30%) for 45 minutes approximately, until it is tender and flaky.

trout Any of several varieties (brown or river, rainbow or sea trout) of fatty, freshwater or saltwater **fish** of the salmon family. Rainbow trout are now farmed on an extensive scale and are available all the year round. When buying fresh trout always look for firm fish with bright pink flesh. They are usually cooked and served gutted and whole, but trout fillets can be bought.

TO COOK: wash and dry a whole fish and slash the skin down the sides of the body to prevent it bursting during cooking. Place into a buttered dish, add a little lemon juice and **shield** the tail with small pieces of **foil**. Cover the dish and cook 2, 225 g trout on high for 5–6 minutes, and 4 for 7–8 minutes. Turn the fish over and rearrange halfway through cooking. Allow them to **stand** for 3 minutes. Scatter over toasted almond flakes and serve.

tuna Any of various large, marine, fatty **fish**. Tuna is commonly sold in cans, but it is becoming more widely available fresh and cut into steaks.

TO COOK: brush the steaks with oil and wrap individually in greaseproof paper. Place them on a plate and cook 450 g of tuna on high for 4 minutes, turning the steaks halfway through cooking. Allow to **stand** for 3 minutes. Canned tuna may be used in a variety of dishes that can be cooked in the microwave.

turbot A large, European flatfish, which is sold either whole or as fillets or steaks. Turbot has firm, white succulent flesh, which is tender and moist when cooked. It is considered to be the finest flatfish. Smaller ('chicken') turbot are also available, which weigh 1–1.4 kg and have a finer texture and taste.

TO COOK: place the steaks on a buttered dish and sprinkle with a little dry white wine. Cover the dish and cook 450 g of turbot on high for 4–5 minutes. Allow to **stand** for 2 minutes.

turkey A domestic fowl, of North American origin, and its meat. Turkeys are available both

fresh and frozen, and the hen is considered to
be more tender than the male bird. The size of
the bird will depend on the size of the oven
cavity of the microwave used. It is best not to
exceed 5.5 kg, because anything larger than this
will be difficult to re-position and may not cook
evenly.

Stuff the neck cavity, fold the skin over,
securing it with wooden cocktail sticks, and tie
the legs and wings with string. Brush the skin
with melted butter.

TO COOK: either (a), stand the turkey on a
roasting dish and cover with a split **roasting
bag**; or (b), place it in a roasting bag and tie the
ends loosely and begin cooking it breast-side
down. Cook on high, allowing 8–9 minutes per
450 g and turn the bird over 3 or 4 times during
cooking. **Shield** the thinner more exposed parts
that appear to be overcooking. Allow it to
stand for 20 minutes.

turmeric The aromatic, yellow-coloured
underground stem of a tropical Asian plant
used as a **spice**.

turning food A procedure that ensures that
all parts of a food are exposed evenly to the
microwave energy. It is particularly important
to turn denser foods, such as baked potatoes,
cakes and joints of meat. They should be
turned round and over halfway through
cooking.

turnip A white or yellowish root **vegetable** with a distinctive flavour. Choose firm, clean, unblemished turnips, which are heavy for their size and preferably with their green leaves still attached. Turnips may be cooked then mashed and used in soups, stews and casseroles.

To prepare, wash thoroughly and peel, leave smaller ones whole, but cut larger ones into segments, chunks, slices or julienne strips.

TO COOK: put 450 g of prepared turnips into a dish and add 3 tbsp of water. Cover the dish and cook on high for 8–10 minutes, until tender, stirring twice. Allow to **stand** for 2 minutes and then drain well.

turntable A feature of most microwave ovens that promotes even cooking and eliminates (for most dishes) the need to rotate the food, although food will still have to be rearranged. Most turntables can be switched off when cooking large, awkwardly shaped dishes that would jam against the oven sides. Those models without a turntable will be fitted with a **rotating antenna** to distribute the microwave energy.

two-level oven A microwave oven that has a shelf that allows food to be cooked on two levels. A two-level oven allows a greater degree of flexibility if several foods need to be cooked at the same time, but it does require careful planning and accurate cooking times. In these ovens about 60% of the microwave energy is fed to the upper section and 40% to the lower part.

uncovering food It is safer to remove the covers of cooked foods, such as lids or clingfilm, towards you. The escaping steam is very hot and could easily cause scalds.

utensil See **microwave tools**.

vanilla The dark, aromatic pod of certain varieties of tropical orchid, used as a flavouring. Vanilla pods have no flavour when they are picked because the flavour develops during the curing process. Vanilla extract can be bought in bottles and the pods whole. The pods may be stored in a jar of sugar. A whole pod may be used to flavour custards and other liquids.

To flavour milk allow one pod per 600 ml. Put into a jug and heat on high for 2–3 minutes until boiling. Allow to **stand** until cool. Remove the pod, rinse in cold water and dry it on kitchen paper, it can then be used again.

variable power control A facility available on many models of microwave ovens. It provides a range of cooking power levels from high through medium to low, with anything up to ten different settings. Variable power provides greater control over heating or cooking.

However, power levels have not been standardized and they vary from model to model. The setting may also be represented in different ways, by numbers, percentages, wattage or by cooking methods. The control may be a dial or a touch control incorporated into the same panel as the timing control. In some models, unless an alternative to high power is programmed the microwave may operate on high automatically.

veal   The flesh of a calf fed exclusively on milk or other foods low in iron. Veal is very lean and because of its immaturity it has very little connective tissue or a strong flavour. Choose veal that is pale pink and has very little fat.

TO COOK: joints, such as loin, leg and shoulder joints on the bone, benefit from marinating. After marinating drain and place on a **roasting dish**, fat-side down, inside a **roasting bag**. Cook on high for 8–9 minutes per 450 g and turn over halfway through cooking. Boned and rolled joints should be cooked for 9–10 minutes per 450 g. Allow to **stand** for 15 minutes.

To test if the meat is properly cooked use a microwave thermometer. The temperature should be 65°C (150°F) when the meat is taken out of the oven, rising to 75°C (170°F) during the standing time.

Veal loin chops and cutlets are best browned on a pre-heated **browning dish**. Add 2 tbsp of oil and arrange the narrow ends towards the centre. Cook 2, 175 g chops on high for 6–8 minutes, turning them over after a third of the cooking time. Cover and allow to **stand** for 2–3 minutes.

Escalopes of veal are very tender and are usually beaten until very thin. Pre-heat a browning dish, add 2 tbsp of oil and 15 g of butter. Add 450 g of escalopes, press them down and then cook each side on high for 1 minute. Then continue to cook them on medium for a further 2–3 minutes.

For stews use pie veal, which should be cooked slowly with vegetables and stock. For 450 g of meat cook on high for the first 10 minutes and then continue on medium for 35 minutes until tender, stirring during cooking. Allow to stand for 5 minutes.

Knuckle or shin is sold cut up to be braised to make Osso Bucco. Cook 1 kg of veal on high for the first 10 minutes and then on medium for 20–25 minutes. Allow to stand for 10 minutes. See also **beef**.

vegetable The edible leaves, fruit, roots, flowers or stalks of plants. Most vegetables cook very successfully in the microwave. Because they are cooked quickly they retain their colour, flavour and nutrients well. For the best results use fresh vegetables and cut them into uniform-sized pieces so that they are cooked evenly. Frozen vegetables need only a very small amount of water. Always pierce whole vegetables with skins to prevent them from bursting. If properly cooked the vegetables should be firm but tender. If overcooked they may go soft, dry out or harden.

See **asparagus**; **aubergine**; **avocado pear**; **beansprout**; **broccoli**; **Brussels sprout**; **cabbage**; **cauliflower**; **celery**; **chicory**; **Chinese leaf**; **courgette**; **fennel**; **globe artichoke**; **kale**; **marrow**; **mushroom**; **onion**; **pumpkin**; **salsify**; **shallot**;

spinach; **spring greens**; **sweet potato**; **sweetcorn**; **tomato**; **watercress**.

vegetable oil   See **oil**.

vegetable squash   See **spaghetti squash**.

venison   The flesh of deer. Good venison should be dark red with a fine grain and firm white fat. Like beef some cuts are more suitable for microwaving than others. Haunch and loin are prime roasting cuts, but shoulder is usually casseroled. Marinating venison gives flavour and helps to tenderize the meat. Venison is a dry meat and when roasting a joint it will need added fat to keep it moist.

TO COOK: for a roasting joint, marinate it for 12–48 hours before cooking. Take out of the marinade and brush it with oil and then place it in a pierced **roasting bag**. Put it in a dish and cook on high for 7–9 minutes per 450 g. Allow to **stand** for 15 minutes.

vine leaf   The young, tender leaf of the grape vine, which is available fresh in the summer and autumn. Vine leaves need to be blanched for a few minutes to soften them before use. Those that have been canned or packed in brine need to be thoroughly rinsed in warm water. They are used as edible wrappings for other foods.

warm A microwave power setting. The warm setting is used for keeping foods warm for up to 30 minutes. It is also useful for softening some foods, such as butter, cream cheese, for melting chocolate, proving yeast and for very gentle cooking. On the warm setting the energy is on for approximately 25% of the time. The power level is about 120–150 W and it may be numbered 1 or 2 or called low.

water Foods with a high water content, such as tomatoes, can be cooked in the microwave without any added liquid because water attracts microwave energy.

water chestnut The succulent corm of a Chinese plant about the size of a walnut, traditionally used in Chinese cookery. Although they are commonly available in cans they may also be bought fresh from Chinese food shops. The fresh ones are tastier than the canned ones and can be stored, unpeeled, in the refrigerator for 2 weeks. Canned ones keep for up to a week in the refrigerator (transferred to a non-metallic container), but the water must be changed daily.

To prepare water chestnuts, peel with a sharp knife and trim the root and stem to give a thick disc. They are used in salads, vegetable dishes and spicy stir-fries. They are also finely diced and added to stuffings and fillings.

watercress A leafy green vegetable grown in fresh, running water. Watercress is used in salads, as a garnish and, because of its peppery flavour, it is excellent in soups and sauces. Choose short sprigs with crisp deep-green stems and firm, well-coloured leaves. It should be washed thoroughly before use.

wattage The power rating of an electrical appliance. A microwave oven has two energy ratings in watts (W) or kilo watts (kW). The first rating refers to input, which is the total amount of energy consumed. The second rating refers to the output, which is the maximum amount of microwave energy produced for cooking. Obviously, the higher the output the more powerful the oven. Most domestic ovens have outputs of between 500–700 W. Check the wattage of the oven before following a recipe, because most recipes and convenience foods have been tested in 650 W ovens.

wave guide A device that directs the high frequency microwaves produced by the **magnetron** into the oven cavity, and is helped by the **stirrer fan**.

wave stirrer See **stirrer fan**.

whisking During cooking whisking keeps a sauce smooth and helps to ensure that it is cooked evenly. A microwave whisk has a bent handle so that it can be left in the bowl during cooking.

whiting   A white **fish** related to the cod, which is usually sold as fillets.

TO COOK: arrange the fillets in a dish with the thin ends overlapping or folded under. Add 2–3 tbsp of wine (if preferred), season and cover the dish. Cook 225 g on high for 3 minutes, rearranging once during cooking. Allow to **stand** for 2 minutes.

wholewheat   Wheat that has not been refined by processing. Wholewheat is available in a variety of forms, including whole grains, kibbled wheat, wheatflakes and flours. See also **bulgar wheat**; **couscous**; **semolina**.

wine   An alcoholic drink usually made by fermenting grapes. Wine can be used in small quantities in the microwave, too much, however, may ignite. See also **alcohol**.

Worcestershire sauce   A thin, black-brown sauce that is made through a process of marinading and blending. Worcestershire sauce may be used extensively in cooking to add flavour to soups, stocks and sauces. It is equally good with fish, poultry, game and meat. Used sparingly it can be brushed lightly onto beef, pork or lamb cuts to help brown them.

wrapping food Some foods benefit from being wrapped in **kitchen paper** while they are cooked, so that the moisture produced on the surface of the food is absorbed, for example **baked potatoes**.

yam The starchy tuber of any of various tropical, twining plants. Yams have brown, woody skins and moist, sweet flesh. They come in a variety of shapes and sizes, and may be used in casseroles or served with other vegetables in spicy sauces. Choose firm, undamaged yams with regular shapes.

TO COOK: to prepare, wash, peel and dice. Put 450 g of prepared yams into a dish with 3 tbsp of water. Cover the dish and cook on high for 8–10 minutes, stirring once. Allow to **stand** for 3 minutes.

yeast dough Although bread does not bake successfully in the microwave, with care the yeast dough can prove. Place a jug of hot water in the microwave, put the dough into a bowl and cover it with kitchen paper, then place the bowl beside the jug. Heat 675 g on low or minimum power for 4 minutes. The dough will be ready when it has doubled its size.

yeast extract A savoury paste, which is used as a spread and may be added to soups and stews to add flavour.

yoghurt A thick, custard-like dairy product made by curdling milk with certain strains of bacteria. A microwave oven with a **temperature probe** can be used to make yoghurt.

TO MAKE: heat the milk to 45°C (112°F) and
stir in 1 tbsp of live yoghurt. Keep the milk
warm and still until set.

zucchini See **courgette**.

Appendix I
Cooking Tables

The tables are divided into the following sections: Eggs; Fish & Shellfish; Fruit; Grains & Rice; Meat; Offal; Pasta; Poultry & Game; Pulses; Vegetables. The cooking times given are for cooking on high (unless otherwise stated) in a 650 W oven.

EGGS	QUANTITY	COOKING TIME	NOTES
Egg, fried	1 2 3	$\frac{1}{2}$–1 min 1–1$\frac{1}{2}$ min 2–2$\frac{1}{2}$ min	Always pierce the egg yolks before cooking.
Egg, poached	1 2 4	$\frac{1}{2}$–1 min 1–1$\frac{1}{2}$ min 2$\frac{1}{2}$–3 min	Cook in a lightly greased ramekin, dot with butter. Turn the dish halfway through cooking.
Egg, scrambled	2 4	1$\frac{1}{2}$–2 min 3$\frac{1}{2}$–4 min	Beat 2 eggs with 2 tbsp of milk. Stir 3 or 4 times.

FISH & SHELLFISH	QUANTITY	COOKING TIME	NOTES
breaded/battered fillets	225 g 450 g	3–4 min 5–6 min stand 2 min	Cook on pre-heated browning dish, arrange in single layer turn over halfway.
fillets (thick) e.g. cod, coley, haddock, hake.	225 g 450 g	2 min 2–3 min stand 2 min	Overlap thin ends towards centre, or fold tails under.
fillets (thin) e.g. plaice, sole, whiting.	225 g 450 g	2 min 2–3 min stand 2 min	Arrange in a single layer, skin side down. Tails overlapping or folded.
herring roe (soft)	225 g	2 min stand 1 min	Cook in butter, turning once.

FISH & SHELLFISH	QUANTITY	COOKING TIME	NOTES
kipper	225 g	3–4 min stand 2 min	Place skin side down on a rack, or a buttered dish. Cover with grease-proof paper, turn over halfway.
mussels (in shell)	1 kg	4–5 min stand 3 min	Discard cracked shells & shells still closed after cooking.
prawns, scampi and shrimps.	225 g 450 g	1½–2 min 3–4 min	Shell & de-vein before or after cooking. Cook in a single layer and stir.
skate wings	450 g 1 kg	4 min 7–8 min stand 3 min	Cut large wings into wedges; thinner tips to the centre, turn once.

FISH & SHELLFISH	QUANTITY	COOKING TIME	NOTES
smoked fish e.g. cod.	225 g 450 g	2½–3 min 3–4 min stand 3 min	Cook in pierced roasting bag, rearrange halfway.
steaks e.g. halibut.	225 g 450 g	3 min 4 min stand 1–2 min	Thin ends to the centre, cover with greaseproof paper, rearrange during cooking.
whole fish (round) e.g. bass, trout.	225 g 450 g	3–4 min 4–6 min stand 3 min	Slash skins 2 or 3 times; shield head & tail with foil.
whole fish (flat) e.g. plaice, sole.	225 g 450 g	2 min 2–3 min stand 2 min	Skin, brush with butter, shield tail with foil. Cook singly.

FRUIT	QUANTITY	COOKING TIME	NOTES
Apple (fresh slices)	225 g 450 g	3–4 min 5–6 min	Sprinkle with a little lemon juice & sugar.
Apple (frozen slices)	450 g	8–10 min	
Apple (whole)	1 medium 2 medium 4 medium	2–3 min 4–5 min 7–9 min	Rotate apples halfway through cooking.
Banana	2 medium 3–4 medium	2–3 min 3–4 min	Cut into thick slices, add a little lemon juice & sugar, rearrange halfway.
Berries	450 g	4–5 min	Top & tail or hull, add 100 g of sugar.

FRUIT	QUANTITY	COOKING TIME	NOTES
Dried fruit	225 g	10–12 min stand 10–30 min	Add 600 ml of boiling liquid.
Pear	225 g 450 g	3–4 min 5–7 min	Use 300 ml of cider or red wine & 100 g of sugar. Allow the fruit to cool in the syrup.
Rhubarb (fresh)	450 g	7–8 min stand 3 min	Cut into short lengths, add 3 tbsp of water & 100 g of sugar.
Rhubarb (frozen)	450 g	9–10 min	

FRUIT	QUANTITY	COOKING TIME	NOTES
Soft fruit	450 g	4–5 min	Cook whole or halve & stone. Cook in syrup or sprinkle with 100 g of sugar.

GRAINS & RICE	QUANTITY	COOKING TIME	NOTES
Bulgar	100 g	2–3 min stand 5 min	Add 300 ml of boiling water.
Cornmeal, polenta	100 g	5–8 min stand 10–15 min	Add 600 ml of boiling water or stock. Add 25 g of butter at the end of cooking.
Couscous	100 g	2–3 min stand 5 min	Add 300 ml of boiling water.
Oatmeal, porridge	3 tbsp per serving	3½–4 min stand 2 min	200 ml of liquid & stir well.
Rice, brown	225 g	25–30 min stand 5 min	Add 750 ml of boiling water.
Rice, white	225 g	10 min stand 5 min	Add 600 ml of boiling water.

MEAT	QUANTITY	COOKING TIME	NOTES
Bacon (joint)	450 g 1 kg	13–15 min 16–20 min stand 10 min	Soak in cold water for several hours, drain, place in pierced roasting bag & stand on a rack. Turn over during cooking.
Bacon (rashers)	1 rasher 2 rashers 4 rashers	30–45 sec 1–1½ min 2–2½ min	Place on a plate or bacon rack & cover with kitchen paper.
Bacon (steaks)	175 g 450 g	4 min 7 min stand 2 min	Snip the fat at intervals, cook on a bacon rack, cover with kitchen paper & turn over once.

MEAT	QUANTITY	COOKING TIME	NOTES
Beef (joint with bone)	450 g	6–8 min then on medium for rare: 5–6 min medium: 6–7 min well done: 7–9 min stand 15 min	Place on a rack in a pierced roasting bag. Turn over and around during cooking. Tent in foil while standing.
Beef (joint boned & rolled)	450 g	rare: 5–6 min medium: 7–8 min well done: 8–10 min stand 15–20 min	Cook as for joint on the bone.

MEAT	QUANTITY	COOKING TIME	NOTES
Braising steak	450 g	5 min then on medium for 45 min stand 10 min	Stir during cooking.
Minced beef	450 g	7–8 min	Add 2–3 tbsp of water & stir to break up lumps.
Beefburgers	1 × 100 g 2 × 100 g	3 min 4–5 min	Use a browning dish, turn over halfway.

MEAT	QUANTITY	COOKING TIME	NOTES
Lamb (joint with bone)	450 g	medium: 6–8 min well done: 7–9 min stand 15 min	Protect bony end with foil. Place on a rack in a pierced roasting bag. Turn over & round during cooking.
Lamb (joint boned)	450 g	medium: 9 min well done: 10 min stand 15 min	Cook as for joint on the bone.
Lamb casserole	450 g	5–7 min then on medium for 20 min stand 10 min	Stir twice during cooking.

MEAT	QUANTITY	COOKING TIME	NOTES
Lamb chops (chump, steaks, neck cutlets & noisettes)	450 g	medium: 5–6 min well done: 7–9 min stand 4–5 min	Use a browning dish to improve colour. Arrange in a single layer, bony end towards the centre. Turn over halfway & stir during cooking.
Lamb – Crown Roast	450 g	9–10 min stand 20 min	Reposition during cooking.
Lamb kebabs	450 g	6–8 min	Turn over halfway.
Lamb stew	450 g	5 min then on low for 50–60 min	Stir during cooking.

MEAT	QUANTITY	COOKING TIME	NOTES
Lamb, rack of (best end of neck)	450 g	medium: 6–7 min well done: 7–9 min stand 10–15 min	Cook as a joint.
Pork (joint with bone)	450 g	9–10 min stand 15–20 min	Rub a little oil & salt into skin, cook as for lamb or beef joint.
Pork (joint boned)	450 g	10–12 min stand 15–20 min	Rub a little oil & salt into skin, cook as for lamb or beef joint.
Pork chops (loin, chump)	2 chops 4 chops	4 min 6 min stand 3 min	Best cooked in a browning dish. Place with bone ends towards centre. Turn over once.

MEAT	QUANTITY	COOKING TIME	NOTES
Pork braised	450 g	6–8 min then on medium for 7–9 min stand 20 min	Flavour with a little cider.
Pork spareribs	450 g	5 min then on medium for 5 min stand 5 min	Cook on a roasting rack, drain off fat halfway, turn over & brush with a marinade or sauce.
Sausages	225 g 450 g	4–5 min 6–7 min	Prick skins. Use a browning dish or brush with a browning agent. Rearrange & turn during cooking.

MEAT	QUANTITY	COOKING TIME	NOTES
Veal (joint with bone)	450 g	8–9 min stand 15 min	Place on a rack, fat-side down & inside a pierced roasting bag. Turn over halfway.
Veal (joint, boned & rolled)	450 g	9–10 min stand 15 min	Cook as for veal joint on the bone.
Veal escalopes	225 g	2–3 min	Use a browning dish for the best results.
Veal stew	450 g	10 min then on medium for 35 min stand 5 min	Stir during cooking.

OFFAL	QUANTITY	COOKING TIME	NOTES
Brains (calf or lamb)	450 g	6–8 min then on medium for 10–12 min *plus 3–8 min	Soak in cold water for 30 min. After first part of cooking slice bread-crumb & cook in a browning dish*.
Heart	450 g	45 min (medium) stand 10 min	Best cut up and cooked slowly in a stew.
Kidney (lamb & pig)	225 g 450 g	3–4 min 6–8 min stand 3 min	Prick membrane, halve and remove the white core.
Liver (lamb)	225 g 450 g	3–4 min 6–7 min stand 3 min	Remove skin & tough membranes. Cook in a browning dish.

OFFAL	QUANTITY	COOKING TIME	NOTES
Oxtail	1 kg	6–8 min then on medium for 1 hour stand 10 min	Cook in a browning dish for the first stage, then in a casserole.
Sweetbread (calf & lamb)	450 g	8–10 min stand 10 min	Soak for a few hours, then blanch before cooking.
Tongue (ox)	1 kg	high until boiling then on medium for 65–70 min stand 10 min	Soak before cooking.

PASTA	QUANTITY	COOKING TIME	NOTES
Pour in enough boiling water to cover the pasta and stir well during cooking. Large quantities of pasta are best cooked conventionally.			
Fresh, white wholemeal or spinach	225 g	1–2 min	
Dried shapes, white, wholemeal or spinach	225 g 450 g	6–8 min 10–12 min stand 5 min	
Dried spaghetti	225 g	7–8 min	
Dried tagliatelle	450 g	7 min	
Lasagne sheets	225 g	8–10 min stand 5 min	

POULTRY & GAME	QUANTITY	COOKING TIME	NOTES
Chicken (whole)	450 g	7–9 min (medium) stand 15 min	Brush skin with browning agent in a roasting bag, turn over & round during cooking.
Chicken (portions with bone)	225 g 450 g	4–5 min 6–8 min stand 5 min	Arrange in a single layer with thinner ends towards the centre.
Chicken (boneless)	225 g 450 g	3½–4 min 5–6 min stand 5 min	Skin-side up with thinner parts towards the centre, rearrange halfway.
Duck (whole)	1.75 kg	28 min stand 15 min	Prick the skin. Drain off juices after first 10 min.

POULTRY & GAME	QUANTITY	COOKING TIME	NOTES
Duck (portions with bone)	300 g (four)	20 min stand 10 min	Position & rearrange as for chicken.
Duck (breast)	2 portions 4 portions	4–5 min 6–8 min stand 3–5 min	Brush with a little butter, cook in a single layer. Turn over halfway.
Game (e.g. grouse or partridge)	450 g	7–9 min stand 5 min	Wrap breast with bacon or smear with butter to keep moist. Cook in a roasting bag.

POULTRY & GAME	QUANTITY	COOKING TIME	NOTES
Goose	450 g	7 min stand 20 min	Prick skin, place breast-side down in a split roasting bag. Drain off fat & turn over halfway.
Hare (joints)	450 g	12–15 min (medium) stand 5 min	Turn over & rearrange during cooking.
Rabbit (joints)	450 g	5 min then 15 min on medium stand 5 min	Turn over & rearrange during cooking.

POULTRY & GAME	QUANTITY	COOKING TIME	NOTES
Turkey (whole; 3–5 kg/6–10 lb)	450 g	8–9 min stand 15–20 min	Turn over 3–4 times, depending on size. If breast starts to over-cook protect it.
Turkey (joint, boned & rolled)	450 g	8–9 min stand 15–20 min	Remove outer wrapping, leave on inner paper. Place in a pierced roasting bag. Turn over & round during cooking.
Turkey (escalopes)	225 g	4–5 min stand 2 min	Cook on a browning dish, turn over after one-third of cooking time.

POULTRY & GAME	QUANTITY	COOKING TIME	NOTES
Venison	450 g	7–9 min stand 15 min	Marinate 12–48 hours. Drain & place in a pierced roasting bag. Turn over & around halfway.

PULSES	QUANTITY	COOKING TIME	NOTES
Note that all pulses double in weight when cooked. Soak the beans overnight, then drain. Pour over enough boiling water to cover the beans and cook covered, stirring occasionally.			
Adzuki bean	225 g	25–30 min stand 15–20 min	
Black-eyed bean	225 g	20–30 min stand 5–10 min	
Black & Red kidney beans	225 g	20–30 min stand 5–10 min	Ensure that they are boiling for the first 10 minutes.
Borlotti bean	225 g	20–30 min stand 5–10 min	

PULSES	QUANTITY	COOKING TIME	NOTES
Chickpea	225 g	45–50 min stand 5–10 min	Ensure that they are boiling for the first 10 minutes.
Flageolet	225 g	20–30 min stand 5–10 min	
Haricot bean	225 g	20–30 min stand 5–10 min	Ensure that they are boiling for the first 10 minutes.
Lentils (brown or green)	225 g	20–25 min stand 10–15 min	Rinse, removing any grit or stones. Do not need to be soaked overnight.

PULSES	QUANTITY	COOKING TIME	NOTES
Lentils (red split)	225 g	10–12 min stand 5–10 min	As for brown or green lentils.
Mung bean	225 g	20–25 min stand 10 min	
Split pea	225 g	15–20 min stand 5–10 min	Do not need to be soaked overnight.

VEGETABLE	QUANTITY	COOKING TIME	NOTES
Fresh vegetables need very little water to cook in. Unless otherwise stated add 3–4 tbsp of water and cook in a covered dish, stirring or rearranging during cooking. Frozen vegetables require no added liquid. Once cooked most vegetables need to stand for 2 minutes.			
Asparagus (fresh)	225 g 450 g	6–7 min 7–9 min	Arrange thicker stems towards the outside of the dish.
Asparagus (frozen)	225 g 450 g	7–8 min 11–12 min	
Aubergine (fresh)	225 g 450 g	3–4 min 5–7 min stand 3–4 min	Cut into cubes or slices.

VEGETABLE	QUANTITY	COOKING TIME	NOTES
Beansprout (fresh)	225 g	2 min	Should still be crisp after cooking.
Beetroot (fresh, baby)	225 g 450 g	9–12 min 12–18 min stand 5 min	Peel after standing time & when cool enough to handle.
Broad bean (fresh)	225 g 450 g	5–6 min 7–8 min	
Broad bean (frozen)	225 g 450 g	7–8 min 10–12 min	

VEGETABLE	QUANTITY	COOKING TIME	NOTES
Broccoli (fresh)	225 g 450 g	4–5 min 7–8 min stand 2 min	Rearrange during cooking.
Broccoli (frozen)	225 g 450 g	7–8 min 10–12 min	
Brussels sprout (fresh)	225 g 450 g	4–5 min 7–8 min stand 2 min	Slit stems & cut larger ones in half.
Brussels sprout (frozen)	225 g 450 g	6–7 min 8–10 min	
Cabbage (fresh)	225 g 450 g	2–4 min 5–7 min	Cook red cabbage a little longer.

VEGETABLE	QUANTITY	COOKING TIME	NOTES
Cabbage (frozen)	225 g 450 g	5 min 7 min	
Carrot (fresh)	225 g 450 g	5–6 min 6–8 min	Small, whole carrots may take a little longer than slices.
Carrot (frozen)	225 g 450 g	5–6 min 6–8 min	
Cauliflower (fresh)	225 g 450 g	4–5 min 6–8 min	Cut into even-size florets.
Cauliflower (frozen)	225 g 450 g	4–5 min 6–7 min	

VEGETABLE	QUANTITY	COOKING TIME	NOTES
Celeriac (fresh)	225 g 450 g	5–7 min 8–10 min	Cut into slices or julienne.
Celery (fresh)	225 g 450 g	5–6 min 6–7 min	Cut into 2 cm slices.
Corn on the cob (fresh)	2 4	6–7 min 8–9 min	Remove leaves & silky threads. Turn over & rearrange halfway.
Corn on the cob (frozen)	2 4	7–8 min 10–12 min	
Corn, baby (fresh)	225 g	3–4 min	

VEGETABLE	QUANTITY	COOKING TIME	NOTES
Corn, baby (frozen)	225 g	5–6 min	
Courgette (fresh)	225 g 450 g	4–5 min 6–7 min	Do not add any water.
Courgette (frozen)	225 g 450 g	5–6 min 7–8 min	
Fennel (fresh)	225 g 450 g	4–5 min 6–8 min	Cut in half or quarters.
French bean (fresh)	225 g 450 g	5–6 min 7–8 min	
French bean (frozen)	225 g 450 g	6–8 min 8–9 min	

VEGETABLE	QUANTITY	COOKING TIME	NOTES
Globe artichoke	1	5–6 min	Cook in a roasting bag, stand upright to cook & rotate once during cooking.
	2	7–8 min	
	4	12–13 min	
Kohlrabi (fresh)	450 g	7–9 min	Slice or dice.
Leek (fresh)	225 g	4–5 min	Slice.
	450 g	6–8 min	
Leek (frozen)	225 g	5–6 min	
	450 g	6–8 min	
Mangetout (fresh)	225 g	3–4 min	Top & tail, add a little butter instead of water.

VEGETABLE	QUANTITY	COOKING TIME	NOTES
Mangetout (frozen)	225 g	4–5 min	
Marrow (fresh)	450 g	5–7 min	Cut into cubes.
Mixed vegetables (frozen)	225 g 450 g	6–7 min 9–10 min	
Mushroom (fresh)	100 g 225 g	$1\frac{1}{2}$–2 min 2–3 min stand 1 min	If fresh, wipe clean but do not wash.
Mushroom (frozen)	100 g	2–$2\frac{1}{2}$ min	

VEGETABLE	QUANTITY	COOKING TIME	NOTES
Okra (fresh)	225 g	4–5 min	Usually cooked whole.
Onion (fresh)	225 g 450 g	2–4 min 5–6 min	Slice or dice.
Parsnips (fresh)	225 g 450 g	5–6 min 8–10 min stand 2–3 min	
Pea (fresh)	225 g	3–4 min stand 3 min	
Pea (frozen)	225 g	5–6 min	

VEGETABLE	QUANTITY	COOKING TIME	NOTES
Petit pois (frozen)	225 g	2–3 min	
Peppers (fresh)	225 g	2–3 min	Cut into slices or rings.
Potatoes (new)	450 g	8–10 min	Prick the skins and cook whole.
Potatoes (old)	450 g	8–10 min	Cut into even-sized pieces.

VEGETABLE	QUANTITY	COOKING TIME	NOTES
Potatoes, baked	1 × 150 g 2 × 150 g 3 × 150 g 4 × 150 g	5 min 6–8 min 9–10 min 10–12 min stand 3 min	Prick skins, place on kitchen paper & turn over halfway through cooking.
Runner bean (fresh)	225 g 450 g	6 min 8–10 min stand 2 min	Top, tail and slice.
Runner bean (frozen)	225 g 450 g	5–6 min 6–8 min	
Spinach (fresh)	225 g 450 g	2–3 min 3–4 min	

VEGETABLE	QUANTITY	COOKING TIME	NOTES
Spinach (fresh – leaf or chopped)	450 g	7–9 min	
Spring greens (fresh)	450 g	6–7 min	
Swede (fresh)	225 g 450 g	7–8 min 8–9 min stand 2 min	Peel thickly & dice.
Swede (frozen)	225 g	4–5 min	
Tomato	1 2	30 sec 1½–2 min	Halve.

VEGETABLE	QUANTITY	COOKING TIME	NOTES
Turnip (fresh)	450 g	8–10 min stand 2 min	Peel & dice.
Turnip (frozen)	225 g	6–7 min	

Appendix II
Thawing Tables

The thawing times given are for defrosting on the Low or Defrost (30%) power setting in a 650 W oven. These tables are divided into the following sections: Bread; Cakes & Pastry; Fish & Shellfish; Meat; Poultry & Game. When defrosting large joints, whole fish or poultry shield the thinner parts (bony ends, tails and wing tips) with small pieces of foil. Use a rack if available and pour off the liquid as the food defrosts.

BREAD	TIME (LOW OR DEFROST)	NOTES
Bread rolls, scones, tea-cakes etc.	15–20 sec/2 25–35 sec/4	Place on kitchen paper. Time carefully. Stand for 2–3 min.

BREAD	TIME (LOW OR DEFROST)	NOTES
Loaf (whole)	4–6 min/small 6–8 min/large	Uncover & place on kitchen paper. Turn over during thawing. Stand for 5–15 min.
Loaf (sliced)	4–6 min/small 6–8 min/large	Thaw in wrapper, but remove any metal tags. Stand for 10–15 min.
Slice of bread	10–15 sec/1 slice 15–18 sec/2 slices 20–25 sec/4 slices	Place on kitchen paper. Time carefully. Stand for 1–2 min.

CAKES & PASTRY	TIME (LOW OR DEFROST)	NOTES
Cakes	30–45 sec/2 small 1–1½ min/4 small	Place on kitchen paper, turn & rearrange. Stand for 5 min.
Cheesecake (cream topped)	1½–2 min/20 cm	Place on a serving plate, rest halfway through & stand 15–30 min.
Cheesecake (fruit topped)	4–5 min/20 cm	As for cream-topped cheesecake.
Choux bun	1–1½ min/4 small	Stand for 20–30 min.

CAKES & PASTRY	TIME (LOW OR DEFROST)	NOTES
Cream éclair	45 sec/2 1–1½ min/4	Stand for 5–10 min. Stand for 15–20 min.
Doughnut (jam)	45–60 sec/2 45/90 sec/4	Place on kitchen paper. Stand for 5 min.
Doughnut (cream)	45–60 sec/2 1–1½ min/4	Place on kitchen paper. Check after half the thawing time. Stand for 10 min.
Fruit pie	4–5 min/20 cm	Stand for 5–10 min.
Gateau	4–5 min/20 cm	Stand for 30 min.

CAKES & PASTRY	TIME (LOW OR DEFROST)	NOTES
Shortcrust & puff pastry	1 min/225 g packet 2 min/450 g packet	Stand for 20 min. Stand for 20–30 min.
Sponge cake (with cream)	2–3 min/18 cm	Place on kitchen paper. Test & turn after 1 min. Stand for 5 min.
Sponge cake (with jam)	1–1½ min/18 cm	As for sponge cake with cream.

FISH & SHELLFISH

TIME (LOW OR DEFROST)

NOTES

Separate cutlets, fillets or steaks as soon as possible during thawing. Timing depends on the thickness of the fish.

	TIME (LOW OR DEFROST)	NOTES
Whole round fish (e.g. herring, mackerel or trout)	4–6 min/450 g	Stand for 5 min after each 2–3 min. Very large fish should be left to stand for 10–15 min after every 2–3 min.
Whole flatfish (e.g. plaice or halibut), fish fillets, cutlets or steaks	3–4 min/450 g	Stand for 5 min after each 2–3 min.
Lobster, crab & crab claws	6–8 min/450 g	Stand for 5 min after each 2–3 min.

FISH & SHELLFISH	TIME (LOW OR DEFROST)	NOTES
Crab meat	4–6 min/450 g	Break up the solid block carefully. Stand for 5 min after each 2–3 min.
Prawn, shrimp, scampi & scallops	2–3 min/100 g 3–4 min/225 g	Spread in a shallow layer on a double sheet of kitchen paper. Separate during thawing with a fork and remove pieces as they thaw.

MEAT	TIME (LOW OR DEFROST)	NOTES
Remember to turn over a large piece of meat. If the joint shows signs of cooking allow it to stand for 20 minutes. To test if a joint is properly thawed pierce it with a skewer, which should pass easily through the thickest part.		
Bacon (joint)	4–5 min/450 g	Turn over & around several times. Stand for 30 min.
Bacon (rashers)	2–2½ min/450 g 3–4 min/450 g	Separate rashers as soon as possible. Stand for 5–10 min.

MEAT	TIME (LOW OR DEFROST)	NOTES
Beef (joints on the bone)	10–12 min/450 g	Turn over joint. The meat will still be icy in the centre, but will completely thaw after standing for 1 hour.
Beef (joints – sirloin, topside)	8–10 min/450 g	Turn over regularly during thawing and pause if the meat shows signs of cooking. Stand for 1 hour.
Beef (minced)	6–8 min/450 g	Break up with a fork as the edges start to thaw. Stand for 10 min.

MEAT	TIME (LOW OR DEFROST)	NOTES
Cubed steak	6–8 min/450 g	Stand for 10 min.
Lamb/veal (on the bone)	5–6 min/450 g	As for beef joints on the bone. Stand for 30–45 min.
Lamb/veal (bones, rolled joint)	5–6 min/450 g	As for sirloin or top-side. Stand for 30–45 min.
Lamb/veal (chops)	8–10 min/450 g	Separate during thawing. Stand for 10 min.
Lamb (minced)	6–8 min/450 g	Break up with a fork as the edges start to thaw. Stand for 10 min.

MEAT	TIME (LOW OR DEFROST)	NOTES
Offal – kidney	6–9 min/450 g	Separate during thawing. Stand for 5 min.
Offal – liver	8–10 min/450 g	Separate during thawing. Stand for 5 min.
Pork (on the bone)	7–8 min/450 g	As for beef joints on the bone. Stand for 1 hour.
Pork (boned, rolled joint)	7–8 min/450 g	As for sirloin or topside. Stand for 1 hour.

MEAT	TIME (LOW OR DEFROST)	NOTES
Pork (chops)	8–10 min/450 g	Separate during thawing and arrange in a single layer, with the thinner ends towards the centre. Stand for 10 min.
Pork (tenderloin)	8–10 min/450 g	Stand for 10 min.
Sausages & sausagemeat	3–5 min/450 g	Break up solid blocks & turn over & around. Stand for 15 min.
Steak (sirloin or rump)	7–9 min/450 g	Stand for 10 min.

POULTRY & GAME   TIME (LOW OR DEFROST)   NOTES

Poultry and game should be thawed in its freezer wrapping, which should be pierced and any metal tags removed. During thawing pour off the liquid that collects in the wrapping. Chicken, turkey and duck must be completely thawed before it is cooked. Parts of very large birds start to cook before the thawing is complete, therefore allow 20 minutes standing time halfway through. Turn over and around twice during thawing.

POULTRY & GAME	TIME (LOW OR DEFROST)	NOTES
Chicken or duck (whole)	6–8 min/450 g	Protect the bony wing tips & drum sticks with small pieces of foil. Stand for 30 min.
Chicken, duck, hare and rabbit portions	5–7 min/450 g	Separate during thawing. Stand for 10 min.

POULTRY & GAME	TIME (LOW OR DEFROST)	NOTES
Grouse, pheasant, pigeon, poussin & quail	5–7 min/450 g	
Turkey (whole)	10–12 min/450 g	
Turkey (joint)	15–18 min/450 g	Remove the outer wrapper but leave on inner collar.
Turkey or chicken liver	4–5 min/225 g	Place in a microwave dish, then separate as soon as possible.

Appendix III
Reheating Cooked and Convenience Foods

Always follow the instructions given by the manufacturers of convenience foods. All the timings given in this table are for cooking on high (unless otherwise stated) in a 650 W oven.

FOOD	QUANTITY	COOKING TIME	NOTES
Baby food	1 portion	1–1½ min depending on portion size	Remove the lids. Milk can be reheated in plastic bottles or feeder jugs.
Baked beans	1 portion 2 portions 4 portions	1–1½ min 2–2½ min 3–4 min	Stir during reheating.

FOOD	QUANTITY	COOKING TIME	NOTES
Black pudding	225 g 450 g	3–3½ min 4–5 min	Arrange in a single layer and turn over during cooking.
Canned soup	300 ml	3–4 min	Reheat in a serving bowl and stir.
Canned pasta	400 g	2–3 min	Stir once or twice.
Chops & chicken portions	1 serving 2 servings 4 servings	3–4 min 5–6 min 8–9 min	Arrange in a single layer & rearrange during reheating.
Fish (in sauce)	1 serving 2 servings 4 servings	2–3 min 3–5 min 5½–7 min	Rotate the dish during cooking.

FOOD	QUANTITY	COOKING TIME	NOTES
Frankfurter	1 2 4	30 sec 40 sec 1 min	Pierce the skins.
Kipper	2/175 g	3–4 min	Place with skinside down & dot with butter.
Meat dishes (e.g. stew, casserole etc.)	1 serving 2 servings 4 servings	2½–3½ min 5–7 min 8–10 min	Stir once or twice during reheating.
Oven chips	225 g	3–3½ min	Use a browning dish. Stir the chips once or twice.

FOOD	QUANTITY	COOKING TIME	NOTES
Pizza	1 small	$1\frac{1}{2}$–2 min	Place on an oiled pre-heated browning dish & cook uncovered.
	2 small	3–$4\frac{1}{2}$ min	
	1 large	4–5 min	
Plated meal	1 small	2–3 min	Use stacking rings to heat more than one plate. Turn plates round halfway through.
	2 small	4–5 min	
	1 large	3–4 min	
	2 large	5–6 min	
Quiche	1 slice	1–$1\frac{1}{2}$ min	Arrange points towards centre & cook uncovered.
	2 slices	$1\frac{1}{2}$–$2\frac{1}{2}$ min	
	4 slices	$2\frac{1}{2}$–3 min	
Sliced meat	1 serving	2–3 min	Arrange slices evenly & brush with stock or gravy.
	2 servings	$3\frac{1}{2}$–4 min	
	4 servings	5–7 min	

FOOD	QUANTITY	COOKING TIME	NOTES
Soup, gravy & custard	150 ml	$1\frac{1}{2}$–2 min	Stir during reheating.
	300 ml	$2\frac{1}{2}$–3 min	
	600 ml	4–$5\frac{1}{2}$ min	
Tea, coffee, milk, cocoa & drinking chocolate	1 cup	$1\frac{1}{4}$–2 min	Pour into a microwave-safe cup or mug, heat & stir.
	2 cups	$2\frac{1}{4}$–3 min	
	1 mug	$2\frac{1}{2}$–3 min	
Vegetables	1 portion	30–45 sec	Stir during cooking.
	2 portions	1–$1\frac{1}{2}$ min	
	4 portions	$1\frac{1}{2}$–2 min	

Appendix IV
Guide to Comparative Power Settings

Full or High	650/700 W	100%	7 or 9–10
Medium High/Roast	500/550 W	75%	6 or 7–8
Medium/Bake	400 W	60%	5 or 6
Medium/Simmer	300 W	50%	4 or 5
Medium-Low	250 W	40%	3 or 4
Stew or Braise	250 W	40%	3 or 4
Defrost	200 W	30%	2 or 3
Low/Warm	150 W	25%	1 or 2
Warm	60W	10%	1

Appendix V
Roasting Chart using a Microwave Thermometer

MEAT	REMOVE FROM OVEN AT:	AFTER STANDING
Beef		
rare:	55°C/130°F	60°C/140°F
medium:	65°C/150°F	70°C/160°F
well done:	70°C/160°F	75°C/165°F
Pot Roast	65°C/150°F	70°C/160°F
Meat Loaf	55°C/130°F	60°C/140°F
Lamb		
medium:	70°C/160°F	75°C/165°F
well done:	75°C/165°F	80°C/175°F
Ham	55°C/130°F	60°C/140°F
Pork	75°C/165°F	85°C/185°F
Poultry	80°C/175°F	85°C/185°F
Veal	65°C/150°F	70°C/160°F

Appendix VI
Conversion Table

METRIC		IMPERIAL	METRIC	IMPERIAL
25 g	=	1 oz	150 ml	$\frac{1}{4}$ pint/5 fl oz
50 g	=	2 oz	300 ml	$\frac{1}{2}$ pint/10 fl oz
100 g	=	4 oz	600 ml	1 pint
225 g	=	8 oz	900 ml	$1\frac{1}{2}$ pints
350 g	=	12 oz	1 litre	$1\frac{3}{4}$ pints
450 g	=	1 lb		
1 kg	=	2.2 lb